Contents

ROYAL NAVY
Introduction...........................3-10
Pennant Numbers..................11-12

Submarines
- Vanguard Class...................... 14
- Dreadnought Class................. 16
- Astute Class..........................19
- Trafalgar Class......................21
- Underwater Vehicles.............. 22

Aircraft Carriers
- Queen Elizabeth Class............ 26

Landing Platform Dock
- Albion Class.........................29

Destroyers
- Daring Class (Type 45)............ 31

Frigates
- Type 23 (ASW Variant)............ 33
- Type 23 (GP Variant)............... 36
- City Class (Type 26)................ 37
- Inspiration Clas (Type 31)........ 40

Mine Countermeasures Vessels
- Hunt Clas............................ 42
- Sandown Class...................... 44
- Mine Hunting Drone............... 46
- Mine Countermeasures Systems.. 47

Patrol Vessels
- River II Class........................ 50
- River Class........................... 52
- Coastal Training Craft.............54
- Gibraltar Squadron................. 56

Survey/Support Ships
- Scott Class........................... 57
- Ice Patrol............................ 59
- Inshore Survey......................60
- NavyX Support Vessel............. 61
- NavyX Madfox....................... 62
- Dive Support Boat.................. 63

HMS Victory...........................64

Royal Marine Craft......
Ships for the Future Fleet............... 77

ROYAL FLEET AUXILIARY
Introduction............................... 84
Pennant Numbers........................ 85

Tankers..................................... 86
Stores/Specialist Ships.................. 88

OPERATED FOR MoD
Tanker/Strategic Sealift/Ro-Ro........ 93

SERCO MARINE SERVICES
Introduction............................... 96
Fleet List................................... 97

Tugs... 98
Coastal Craft & Trials Ships........... 107
Fleet Tenders, Multi-Purpose
Vessels & Support Craft............... 109

OTHER VESSELS
Contract Vessels........................ 117
Army Vessels............................ 120
Border Force Vessels.................. 122

THE FLEET AIR ARM
Aircraft of the F.A.A................... 127
Introduction............................. 128
Future Aviation Projects...............141

Military Flying Training System....... 143

WEAPONRY
Weapons of the Royal Navy.......... 149

At the end of the line................. 156

British Warships & Auxiliaries 2024

1

CROWN COPYRIGHT/MOD

HMS Prince of Wales

THE ROYAL NAVY

I start this year's annual *British Warships and Auxiliaries* with Ivory Towers because I fear that people in charge of Britain's naval fleet may be living in the same said structures. Take for example an exchange between Sarah Atherton, sitting on the Defence Select Committee in Parliament and the Chief of the Defence Staff, Admiral Sir Tony Radakin.

Sarah Atherton: *"It is generally accepted that the Royal Navy is very capable of deploying key capabilities with limited platforms as part of a multi-national operation. We have received considerable evidence saying that the Royal Navy is not capable of putting together a whole-force package, which I think we often liken to a Falklands taskforce. Are you concerned that there are so many key players in the defence domain, or ecosystem, who share that opinion?"*

Admiral Sir Tony Radakin: *"You refer to the Falklands scenario, which is one of the few scenarios where we might anticipate fighting on our own, so I think it has an elevation from a military point of view as well as a political and psyche of the nation point of view. When we look at that in terms of the strength of Argentina and the differences now, with the base that we have in the Falklands and our continued presence, with Typhoon, a small Army presence, our ships that are down in the Falklands, and our ability to support that with submarines, carriers and escorts, that is not a concern.*

"This is a Navy that is on the up - a Navy that between 2020 and 2030 becomes a carrier Navy again, that alongside the Air Force goes from fourth generation jets to fifth generation jets, and that then has, by dint of previous investment, 22 ships and submarines coming through. Those straddle some of the workhorses - the solid support RFA ships - to new frigates, Astute-class submarines and also our Dreadnought deterrent. So, I suppose I see it differently. In terms of all the commitments that we are supposed to meet at the moment—this applies across the whole of defence - there are 41 operations ongoing, and all of those are being met."

Sarah Atherton: *"So could we defend the Falklands?"*
Admiral Sir Tony Radakin: *"Absolutely!"*

Whether or not we can defend the Falklands is perhaps a side issue as the Argentine economy is sitting on the edge of an abyss at the present time, but history has a habit of repeating itself. The same situation occurred in late 1981 when the military junta decided that a small quick war would be perfect fillip to quell rising civilian unrest back home.

But for the Admiral to say that the Royal Navy with its dwindling numbers of ships, men, weapons and fuel supplies could defend the Falklands from a sustained and relentless attack from Argentina is presumptuous at best and foolhardy at worst. Those who live in Ivory Towers seem to have the best views of perfect vistas where no troubles can be foreseen. Like a modern day Lord Nelson holding a telescope to his blind eye is Admiral Radakin saying 'I see no ships' to the 21st century. For no ships is central to the debate. Yes, modern warships are more capable and their weapons more lethal, but they can only be in one place at a time and with fewer and fewer available hulls they are in less places, more often than ever before.

When the Sudanese civil war erupted where were the Royal Navy warships to help evacuate stranded British nationals trapped in the country? The nearest units were in the Persian Gulf. Even the quickest response from the Ministry of Defence to get RAF aircraft into the scene took an agonising week to organise and implement and then only a handful of the people in country were taken to safety. In previous crises the Royal Navy was on hand to take people away from danger. Whether it was a shortcoming in intelligence, logistics or planning I don't know, but it doesn't ring well with a public that expects the British armed forces to be there to defend us, to assist us, to protect us and to evacuate us if civil unrest occurs.

In the last year the Royal Navy and Royal Fleet Auxiliary have lost the frigates MONTROSE and MONMOUTH (sister ship WESTMINSTER is in such a poor material shape that her life extension refit was halted as it was deemed uneconomic to continue, her future is yet to be decided), the survey ships ENTERPRISE and ECHO, and the tankers WAVE KNIGHT and WAVE RULER, plus several smaller mine countermeasures vessels have been or are being lined up to be decommissioned and sold abroad. And politicians have the temerity to say that the fleet is getting larger. The fleet is beyond anorexic it's full on bulimic. There is no flesh left to cut and the bones of the skeleton have been scratched to the marrow within.

• CROWN COPYRIGHT/MOD

And this is set against a backdrop of the world waking up to the threat posed by China and Russia, Iran and North Korea, and spending more money on their defences, the United Kingdom government policy is to ram their heads into the sand and pretend everything is fine and will blow over, perhaps helped with some nice, but feeble, diplomatic pressure. As I mentioned history has a way of repeating itself. In 1930s Europe Germany elected a fascist dictator, Italy and Spain did the same. Pressures built until war erupted and the British response was our traditional 'head-in-the-sand' until the 'crap hit the fan' moment and an emergency policy was initiated. In 1938/39 it came just in time to save Britain from being defeated. Today the issues are greater and more complex, but the fundamentals are the same. Tyrants are on the rise in China, Russia, North Korea and Iran and we Brits have our heads between our knees and have adopted the crash position hoping that whatever we have left will be enough to cushion the incoming blow. Sadly, we have cut too far to have a safe, survivable crash landing.

The United States has publicly stated that it considers the withered and old Great Britain to be at best a second rate contributor to NATO, and who could blame them when the British Army has an active force of just 67,000 soldiers, the smallest it has been in four centuries! Some strategists have even gone on record to say that if a full scale war were to erupt, Britain could last 'at best' for just five days before running out of ammunition, supplies, soldiers, airmen, sailors and ships. Yet, Admiral Radakin believes we can defend the Falklands - we can barely defend our own home islands or the fisheries around them let alone a piece of colonial history on the other side of the world.

Submarines
AUKUS is the future. The Australia, UK, USA submarine deal to cover the next thirty to forty years of nuclear submarine development is an amazing piece of politics and business. The basics of the deal is that Australia becomes only the seventh nation on the planet to possess nuclear-powered attack submarines with the assistance from the first and the third to have them. Australia's first nuclear submarines will be three, possibly five, American Virginia Class, probably older vessels, replaced in US Navy service by newer construction. These will be based in a new submarine base being built in Australia again with American and British assistance. From this base American, British and Australian submarines will patrol the Pacific and Indian Oceans. The Virginia's will, however, be only the first step in developing Australia's future undersea capabilities. The existing British SSN(R) programme to design, develop and deliver a successor to the Astute-class submarines is being used as a basis for the AUKUS submarine programme. British and Australian submarines will share a great deal of similarities to enable them to interoperate. American submarines will also share significant amounts of their technologies, sensors, weapons and stealth technologies with their allies to create the perfect attack submarine for the 2030's-2060s. The AUKUS submarines will be built initially at Barrow-in-Furness with the possibility of a second shipyard being constructed from scratch in Australia just for the purpose of building and possibly maintaining the future submarines. In late 2023 contracts worth £4 billion were awarded to BAE Systems, Rolls-Royce and Babcock Marine for the next phase of the SSN-AUKUS submarine programme by the Ministry of Defence. This covers the design, prototyping and purchase of main long lead components for the first UK boats, entering service in the late 2030s.

Dreadnought Submarines

In October 2023 the largest assembly of the first-of-class DREADNOUGHT was wheeled through the streets of Barrow-in-Furness. The giant section of the pressure hull needed to transit from one construction hall to the final assembly hall and the streets of the Cumbrian town, which is now used to the sight of massive sub-assemblies of submarines travelling through the town, witnessed the latest. The Dreadnought programme is proceeding according to schedule and is said to be making good progress with the construction of the three follow-on submarines at various stages of build within the huge BAE buildings in Barrow. Due to the nature of the programme very little information about the submarines has been released to the public.

The submarine fleet will benefit from a four-year £750 million investment into the infrastructure of Devonport Dockyard's submarine refit facilities. The contract signed between Babcock International, and the MoD's Submarine Delivery Agency (SDA) will see a significant upgrading of the site to support future capabilities as they emerge as part of the UK's Defence Nuclear Enterprise. The investment will support enhancements to docks, logistics and new support facilities with an eye to accommodating the largest submarines currently under construction, the Dreadnought Class. It also will assist in the de-activation and de-fuelling of older classes of submarines. The work will centre on 10 Dock within the dockyard and will be undertaken by Costain, Mott MacDonald and Kier BAM.

• CROWN COPYRIGHT/MOD   HMS Forth

Aircraft Carriers

In August 2023 after over a year in Rosyth Dockyard the aircraft carrier PRINCE OF WALES finally returned to sea following the embarrassing propulsion failure en-route to the United States for her first WESTLANT deployment. Now, hopefully, the Royal Navy can focus on the positives of having two operational strike aircraft carriers available for deployment. Sensibly the Ministry of Defence chose to use the time PRINCE OF WALES was in dry-dock to upgrade many of her systems, sensors and propulsion, making her the most up-to-date of the class. These upgrades will, undoubtedly, be added to her sister ship at her next refit period. With two carriers available the Royal Navy has a superb opportunity to show what the Royal Navy can achieve on a global scale and that is exactly what is planned. 2024 will see the two carriers consolidate the work already undertaken to integrate British and Allied F-35B Joint Strike Fighters into its airwing. QUEEN ELIZABETH will in 2024 take part in EXERCISE STEADY DETERMINATION, which is quoted as being 'one of the largest and most important workouts in the NATO Calendar'. PRINCE OF WALES will, however, resume her delayed programme to integrate the F-35Bs during her delayed WESTLANT deployment to the United States. This will put her and her crew in good stead for her planned 2025 UK Carrier Strike Group Global deployment.

Assault ships

There is a persistent rumour that ALBION, now in reserve at Devonport, will be sold before her decommissioning date of 2035. She is a very maintenance intensive vessel even when in reserve, and with only a handful of years left to her service life the idea of selling her off early must be appealing for the bean counters in Whitehall. Brazil is the potential buyer on most people's lips. Whether this sale comes to pass is yet to be seen, but with only one available assault ship (BULWARK) it will leave the Royal Marines with extremely limited resources with which to affect attacks against heavily defended beaches. With the RFA's Bay-class landing docks also expected to leave service within a decade, this is a worrying scenario as future new shipping is still a long way off. There is discussion between the Royal Netherlands Navy and the Royal Navy in how best to approach the replacement programmes as both nations have similarly aged warships and a remarkably similar set of requirements for future LPD/LSDS.

Destroyers

The Royal Navy's six Daring-class destroyers have over the last year been worked hard and have been deployed globally with DAUNTLESS the most high-profile of these deployments having been dispatched to the Caribbean, where she has operated with US and Latin American navies. In this capacity she has interdicted several drug smugglers and caught huge caches of illegal drugs, cutting off the supply to both the United States and Europe. There has been some concern about why a guided missile destroyer that should be used to provide air defence for the fleet is being used in the drug interdiction role, but there is precedent for this as throughout the 1980s-2000s Type 42 destroyers were also similarly deployed. With the Royal Navy's fleet of surface vessels at an all time low, it is not surprising that such a hugely capable vessel as DAUNTLESS would be used in this capacity.

• CROWN COPYRIGHT/MOD

HMS **Prince of Wales**

It is good to report that great progress has been made with the PIP (Propulsion Improvement Programme) across the Type 45 fleet. Most of the six ships have now completed the programme and have had their propulsion systems upgraded to allow them to operate in hot and humid conditions. There is also hope that the planned Ballistic Missile Defence (BMD) capability upgrade for the class will soon be materialised.

Frigates

On 11 July 2023 the first eight crewmembers were assigned to the future HMS VENTURER under construction at Rosyth Dockyard in Scotland. Their presence alongside shipyard workers will directly impact how the ship is built and delivered to the Royal Navy. HMS VENTURER, the first of five Type 31 frigates, is still many years away from being handed over to the Royal Navy and as the years count down more and more Royal Navy personnel will join the ship in build. Work is also progressing, albeit glacially slowly, on the Type 26 frigates. Some naval commentators have commented on how slowly Type 26 build appears to be set against that of the Type 31s and is illusionary as the two Classes should not be compared alongside one another. The Type 31 is a relatively straightforward design that is build with interchangeable blocks, ideal for mass construction, whereas the Type 26 frigates are of a design philosophy altogether and are extremely complex to manufacture. Even with this mind, the delivery of the first of class GLASGOW should not take over a decade to deliver a frigate to the Royal Navy!

At the other end of the frigate life cycle the Type 23 frigate WESTMINSTER appears to be at the end of her career. Scheduled for a refit at Devonport Dockyard the repairs were halted as it became clear that the ship was in an extremely poor materiel state, her future remains unclear as no official word has been issued, but it would make sense not to invest in a refit if it were to cost more than was reasonable. The savings could then be reallocated to other refits that have a greater chance of a satisfactory out-come. It does, however, mean that the Royal Navy will be another frigate short of its already chronically low target for frigates. The rest of the Type 23 frigates are now showing their age, with the youngest of the fleet ST ALBANS already 22 years old. In earlier eras such frigates would have been replaced with new tonnage at around 25 years of age, but in the 21st century warships are now expected to serve for much longer, perhaps too much longer in some cases. The ships are tired and while they have been regularly retrofitted with new propulsion, weapons and sensors, the ships themselves are quite elderly and based on a design formulated in the late 1970s.

MCMV

The move away from manned to autonomous vessels is fast gaining pace with the acquisition of RFA STIRLING CASTLE to act as a mother ship to a growing fleet of small, highly complex unmanned mine countermeasure craft. These specialist vessels have the capacity to effectively control and defeat maritime sea mines in a variety of salinity, depth, inshore and deep-water conditions. As the fleet of autonomous vessels increases the existing legacy hulls of the Sandown and Hunt Classes are being withdrawn from service with the Sandowns scheduled to be decommissioned first, leaving the more complex and capable, yet older, Hunts to remain for a little longer. While removing humans from the dangerous and highly technical task of mine-warfare is to be applauded, it does raise some issues. There is a lack of hulls upon which sailors can cut their teeth, particularly with officers selected for possible future commands. Secondly, the technology, whilst undoubtedly advanced, is still being developed at pace. Should we be throwing out the trusted and dependable Sandowns and Hunts with such undue haste? Should we keep a few in reserve as an insurance against some future unforeseen emergency? After all we are an island dependent on imports for our survival and mines are inexpensive (in military terms) and can be laid in the entrances to major ports almost with impunity.

Patrol

In 2023 there were calls in some quarters for a vastly increased British military presence in Asia and the Pacific as part of former Prime Minister Boris Johnson's eastward shift of focus. Certainly, the Royal Navy, in the vastness of the Pacific Ocean, is a minnow compared against China, Japan, the United States, Australia or even New Zealand. The Royal Navy's 'permanent' presence East of Suez consists of the two River II-class patrol vessels SPEY and TAMAR. Every two years or so, the Royal Navy plans to dispatch a Carrier Strike Group to the region, but can this really be called an increase in British military presence if the carrier and her group of escorts is only in the region for a matter of months? SPEY and TAMAR are doing a sterling job at promoting the Royal Navy and British interests in the region, but it smacks of tokenism. The other patrol vessels of the Class, TRENT, MEDWAY and FORTH continue to operate in their respective forward deployed areas of the Mediterranean and Africa, Caribbean and Falklands and South Atlantic. The earlier River I-class of SEVERN, MERSEY and TYNE provide a very thin line of coastal protection for the United Kingdom in home and European waters.

Survey

With the introduction of new autonomous systems that can be deployed from larger vessels the need for a large fleet of survey ships has been reduced. With the passing from service of ECHO and sister ship ENTERPRISE the Royal Navy's survey fleet now consists of the large SCOTT and the tiny MAGPIE. The Ice Patrol ship PROTECTOR also has a limited surveying capability.

Patrick Boniface
Naval Author &
Editorial Correspondent Warship World

SHIPS OF THE ROYAL NAVY
Pennant Numbers

Ship	P. No.	Page	Ship	P. No.	Page
Aircraft Carriers			*Batch 2*		
QUEEN ELIZABETH	R08	26	*BIRMINGHAM*	*---*	*37*
PRINCE OF WALES	R09	28	*SHEFFIELD*	*---*	*37*
			NEWCASTLE	*---*	*37*
Assault Ships			*LONDON*	*---*	*37*
ALBION	L14	29	*EDINBURGH*	*---*	*37*
BULWARK	L15	29			
			Frigates (Type 31)		
Destroyers (Type 45)			*FORMIDABLE*	*---*	*40*
DARING	D32	31	*BULLDOG*	*---*	*40*
DAUNTLESS	D33	31	*ACTIVE*	*---*	*40*
DIAMOND	D34	31	*VENTURER*	*---*	*40*
DRAGON	D35	31	*CAMPBELTOWN*	*---*	*40*
DEFENDER	D36	31			
DUNCAN	D37	31	**Submarines (Vanguard)**		
			VANGUARD	S28	14
Frigates (Type 23)			VICTORIOUS	S29	14
KENT	F78	33	VIGILANT	S30	14
PORTLAND	F79	33	VENGEANCE	S31	14
SUTHERLAND	F81	33			
SOMERSET	F82	33	**Submarines (Dreadnought)**		
ST ALBANS	F83	33	*DREADNOUGHT*	*---*	*16*
LANCASTER	F229	36	*VALIANT*	*---*	*16*
ARGYLL	F231	36	*WARSPITE*	*---*	*16*
IRON DUKE	F234	36	*KING GEORGE VI*	*---*	*16*
WESTMINSTER	F237	33			
NORTHUMBERLAND	F238	33	**Submarines (Astute)**		
RICHMOND	F239	33	ASTUTE	S119	19
			AMBUSH	S120	19
Frigates (Type 26)			ARTFUL	S121	19
GLASGOW	*F88*	*37*	AUDACIOUS	S122	19
CARDIFF	*F89*	*37*	*AGAMEMNON*	*S123*	*19*
BELFAST	*F90*	*37*	ANSON	S124	19
			AGINCOURT	*S125*	*19*

British Warships & Auxiliaries 2024

Ship	P. No.	Page
Submarines (Trafalgar)		
TRIUMPH	S93	21
Autonomous Underwater Vehicles		
MANTA	S201	22
Minehunters		
LEDBURY	M30	42
CATTISTOCK	M31	42
BROCKLESBY	M33	42
MIDDLETON	M34	42
CHIDDINGFOLD	M37	42
HURWORTH	M39	42
PENZANCE	M106	44
BANGOR	M109	44
Unmanned Minesweepers/Drones		
MINE HUNTING DRONES		46
HEBE	---	47
HARRIER	---	47
HAZARD	---	47
Coastal Training Craft		
EXPRESS	P163	54
EXPLORER	P164	54
EXAMPLE	P165	54
EXPLOIT	P167	54
Patrol Vessel - River II Class		
FORTH	P222	50
MEDWAY	P223	50
TRENT	P224	50
TAMAR	P233	50
SPEY	P234	50
Coastal Training Craft		
ARCHER	P264	54
BITER	P270	54

Ship	P. No.	Page
SMITER	P272	54
PURSUER	P273	54
TRACKER	P274	54
RAIDER	P275	54
BLAZER	P279	54
DASHER	P280	54
Patrol Vessel - River Class		
TYNE	P281	52
SEVERN	P282	52
MERSEY	P283	52
Coastal Training Craft		
PUNCHER	P291	55
CHARGER	P292	55
RANGER	P293	55
TRUMPETER	P294	55
Fast Patrol Boats (Gibraltar Squadron)		
CUTLASS	P295	56
DAGGER	P296	56
Survey Ships & RN Manned Auxiliaries		
MAGPIE	H130	60
SCOTT	H131	57
PROTECTOR	A173	59
NAVYX Support Vessel		
PATRICK BLACKETT	X01	61
NAVYX Unmanned Surface Vessel		
MADFOX	---	62
Dive Support Boats		
VULCAN	---	63
VOLCANO	---	63
ORCADIAN	---	63
CRABB	---	63

Entries displayed in lighter typeface have yet to be completed

Royal Navy Submarines

CROWN COPYRIGHT/MOD

HMS Vanguard

CROWN COPYRIGHT/MOD

VANGUARD CLASS

Ship	Pennant Number	Completion Date	Builder
VANGUARD	S28	1992	VSEL
VICTORIOUS	S29	1994	VSEL
VIGILANT	S30	1997	VSEL
VENGEANCE	S31	1999	VSEL

Displacement: 15,980 tonnes (submerged) **Dimensions:** 149.9m x 12.8m x 12m
Machinery: 1 x Rolls-Royce PWR2 nuclear reactor; 2 GEC Turbines, 27,500 hp; single shaft; pump jet propulsor; two auxiliary retractable propulsion motors **Speed:** 25 + submerged **Armament:** 16 Tubes for Lockheed Trident 2 (D5) missiles, 4 Torpedo Tubes
Complement: 135 (14 officers)

Notes: These four submarines are the second generation of Britain's Independent Nuclear Deterrent. Since 1994, when VANGUARD made her first deployment, this class have performed the silent and little reported role in total secrecy. Each submarine is armed with Trident 2 D5 missiles armed with independent nuclear re-entry vehicles. The number of these re-entry vehicles is being reassessed upwards following the publication of 2021's Integrated Strategic Defence Review.

The submarines are based at Faslane in Scotland and each boat has two captains and two crews which means the duty crew are out while their opposite number are training or on leave. At least one of these submarines are always on patrol somewhere in the world, a second is training and a third is undergoing routine maintenance. The fourth is usually in deep long-term refit or refuelling at Plymouth.

The Vanguard Class are all over 20 years old and will in due course be replaced in service by the new Dreadnought Class currently in build at BAE Systems Shipyard at Barrow-in-Furness. In the meantime, a life extension programme has been initiated to prolong the service careers of VIGILENT and VENGEANCE out to beyond 2028. In mid-May 2023 VANGUARD's epic £500 million refit that started in 2018 was finally completed and the submarine returned to the fleet. The boat's long overhaul and refuel has taken 89 months to complete, compared with her construction at Barrow which lasted just 83 months. VICTORIOUS took her sister ship's place at Devonport at the start of her long overdue refit. The nuclear submarine arrived in Plymouth last year to prepare for the programme which will enable her to continue operational patrols well into the 2030s. Work on VICTORIOUS is already underway. The boat is the second Vanguard-class submarine to undergo a life extension package at Babcock's Devonport facility. She and the rest of the Vanguard fleet are key components in the UK military's longest op - Relentless. Since 1969, at least one nuclear-armed ballistic missile submarine is maintaining the continuous at sea deterrent posture at all times. Babcock and the UK's Submarine Delivery Agency have agreed a contract worth an estimated £560m to deliver the planned deep maintenance and future-proofing of the Vanguard-class boat.

• CROWN COPYRIGHT/MOD

• ROLLS ROYCE

DREADNOUGHT CLASS

Ship	Pennant Number	Completion Date	Builder
DREADNOUGHT	-	-	*BAE Systems (Submarines)*
VALIANT	-	-	*BAE Systems (Submarines)*
WARSPITE	-	-	*BAE Systems (Submarines)*
KING GEORGE VI	-	-	*BAE Systems (Submarines)*

Displacement: 17,200 tonnes (submerged) **Dimensions:** 153.6m **Machinery:** 1 x Rolls-Royce PWR3 nuclear reactor; Turbo-electric drive, pump jet propulsor; single shaft **Speed:** -- **Armament:** 12 x ballistic missile tubes for 8-12 Lockheed Trident II D5 missiles, 4 x 21 inch torpedo tubes for Spearfish heavyweight torpedoes **Complement:** 130

Notes: In May 2011, the Government announced the initial assessment phase for new submarines to replace the Vanguard-class submarines carrying Britain's Independent Nuclear Deterrent. The decision met with vehement objections from anti-nuclear campaigners and even those who objected to the cost of the programme put at £31 billion. At the same time the Government placed orders for long lead time items for the submarines including the nuclear reactors to power them and the specialist high strength steel required to maintain deep diving capabilities. Four years later after the Conservative Party's win at the 2015 elections, the Government committed to maintaining the deterrent with four so called 'Successor' submarines.

As the only shipyard in the United Kingdom able to build complex submarines BAE Systems was contracted to build the first submarine with construction of first of class DREADNOUGHT commencing on 6 October 2016. It is expected that DREADNOUGHT will enter service in 2028 in time to replace VANGUARD which will by then be 30 years old. Construction on the second in class, VALIANT commenced in September 2019.

The DREADNOUGHT Class will have an intended service life longer than the current VANGUARDs at between 35 to 40 years, and will be powered by a nuclear reactor that will not need to be refuelled throughout the operational lifetime of the submarine, greatly reducing maintenance and running costs for the future fleet of four submarines. The missile tubes for the Trident missiles are the same as those being developed for the US Navy's Columbia-class of successor ballistic missile submarines.

The sensors aboard the submarines are expected to be state-of-the-art upon completion and boast items such as second-generation optronic masts instead of traditional periscopes. These masts will be constructed at Govan by Barr and Stroud who have been making submarine periscopes for almost one hundred years.

DREADNOUGHT and her sisters will be the largest submarines ever operated by the Royal Navy, and the most powerful. They also feature separate compartments for male and female personnel, a first on RN submarines. Special lighting arrangements aboard will imitate the day and night on the surface thus making life underwater easier to adapt to for submariners. The submarines will benefit from the installation of 'Fly-by-wire' technology equivalent to systems found on modern airliners. The Active Vehicle Control Management System will oversee all major aspects of the submarines manoeuvring including heading, pitch, depth, and buoyancy. The new system is being developed by BAE Systems Controls and Avionics at their site in Rochester in Kent and will use computers to supplement the work of 'planesmen' operating the submarines, in what is a very physically and mentally demanding role aboard.

Warhead and missile
The UK warhead will be integrated with the US supplied Mark 7 aeroshell to ensure it remains compatible with the Trident II D5 missile and delivered in parallel with the US W93/Mk7 warhead programme. The transition of the current Mark 4 warhead to the Mark 4A is ongoing, addressing obsolescence to ensure the UK continue to have a safe, secure, and available stockpile until the UK replacement warhead is available in the 2030s. The UK also continues to participate with US partners on work to extend the life of the Trident II D5 missiles. These life extension programmes will address obsolescence and continue to provide sufficient missile packages, including spares, to support the UK's current stock entitlement.

International collaboration
In addition to working closely with the US Navy and American authorities the Royal Navy is also collaborating with the French Navy. *"We continue to cooperate with France under the TEUTATES Treaty, signed in November 2010, working together on the technology associated with the nuclear stockpile stewardship in support of our respective independent nuclear deterrent capabilities, in full compliance with our international obligations. Progress continues to be made with the delivery of the experimental hydrodynamic capability at Epure in France and associated capabilities at AWE which*

will allow both the UK and France to conduct independent experiments ensuring both nations' nuclear weapons remain safe and effective."

Reactors and Missile tubes

Rolls-Royce Submarines continue to make good progress with the manufacture of the nuclear propulsion power plants, the Pressurised Water Reactor 3, for all four Dreadnought-class submarines. The procurement on long lead items and other early work for the remaining submarines in the Class, WARSPITE and KING GEORGE VI, continues in line with the overall programme schedule.

As previously reported, production and delivery of the Missile Tubes (MT) to form part of the Common Missile Compartment have been subject to quality shortfalls across the supply chain resulting in their delayed delivery. All 12 missile tubes for HMS DREADNOUGHT have now been delivered to the BAE Systems Barrow shipyard.

CROWN COPYRIGHT/MOD HMS Audacious

• DANIEL FERRO   HMS Audacious

ASTUTE CLASS

Ship	Pennant Number	Completion Date	Builder
ASTUTE	S119	2007	BAE Systems (Submarines)
AMBUSH	S120	2012	BAE Systems (Submarines)
ARTFUL	S121	2015	BAE Systems (Submarines)
AUDACIOUS	S122	2018	BAE Systems (Submarines)
ANSON	S124	2021	BAE Systems (Submarines)
AGAMEMNON	*S123*	*2023*	*BAE Submarine Solutions*
AGINCOURT	*S125*	*2026*	*BAE Submarine Solutions*

Displacement: 7,400 tonnes (7,800 tonnes submerged) **Dimensions:** 97m x 11.2m x 9.5m **Machinery:** Rolls-Royce PWR2; 2 Alsthom Turbines, 27,500 hp; single shaft; pump jet propulsor; two motors for emergency drive; one auxiliary retractable propellor **Speed:** 29+ submerged **Armament:** 6 Torpedo Tubes; Spearfish torpedoes; Tomahawk cruise missiles for a payload of 38 weapons **Complement:** 110 (including 12 Officers)

Notes: This class of nuclear-powered submarines are the direct successors to the extremely successful Trafalgar-class vessels but were designed to incorporate a raft of innovative technologies and systems unheard of when the Trafalgars were in build.

The Astute Class are designed to fulfil a wide-range of strategic and tactical roles within the Royal Navy from anti-ship and anti-submarine warfare, surveillance and intelligence gathering to support of land forces and the delivery of long-range ordnance (Tomahawk cruise missiles) to targets deep within enemy territories. Each submarine has a dock down capability allowing divers to operate from the boat whilst it remains submerged and undetected. This is in addition to the Chalfont dry-deck hangar which can be loaded and unloaded onto the back of the submarines for specialised swimmer teams for stand-off insertion missions for specialist forces.

At the heart of the Astute-class submarines is the BAE Common Combat System (CCS) which was first fully evaluated aboard ARTFUL in February 2016. Essentially the CCS is a computerised brain within the submarine that controls all its sensors in an analogous way to a human nervous system interacts with its ears, eyes, and nose. The system can interpret sonar readings and coordinate appropriate attacks on enemy submarines accordingly. The system was introduced from build on AUDACIOUS and on all new build submarines after that, with retrofitting on older boats at scheduled refit dates.

AUDACIOUS commissioned into service with the Royal Navy on 23 September 2021 following a lengthy build and sea trials programme. The Royal Navy rarely makes public statements about submarine construction programmes. ANSON was accepted into the Royal Navy on 31 August 2022 in the presence of then Prime Minister Boris Johnson and Australian Deputy Prime Minister Richard Marles, who through the AUKUS agreement, have set their sights on building up to ten nuclear powered submarines. Construction of the remaining two Astute-class submarines - AGAMEMNON is expected to be handed over to the Royal Navy in the spring of 2024 and AGINCOURT in 2026. The construction programme for the class has seen significant improvement since the first three vessels were launched.

• CROWN COPYRIGHT/MOD

- CROWN COPYRIGHT/MOD HMS Triumph

TRAFALGAR CLASS

Ship	Pennant Number	Completion Date	Builder
TRIUMPH	S93	1991	Vickers

Displacement: 4,500 tonnes (5,298 tonnes submerged) **Dimensions:** 85.4m x 9.8m x 9.5m **Machinery:** Rolls-Royce PWR1; 2 GEC Turbines, 15,000 hp; single shaft; pump jet propulsor; one motor for emergency drive - retractable propellor **Speed:** 30+ dived **Armament:** 5 Torpedo Tubes; Spearfish torpedoes; Tomahawk cruise missiles for a payload of 24 weapons **Complement:** 130

Notes: TRIUMPH is the last survivor of a class of seven nuclear attack submarines and should, by rights, already have been removed from service, but delays in the Astute Class programme have meant that she has been retained in active service beyond original out of service dates. The Trafalgar Class has, since the mid-1980s, been the backbone of the Royal Navy's silent service, but even in their autumn years the submarines still have a vital role to play in Britain's defence. As hunter-killer submarines, it was their mission to protect first Polaris, now Trident – the country's Strategic Nuclear Deterrent – and to detect, track and classify targets.

The boats are capable of gaining intelligence, covertly inserting troops ashore, or striking at enemy submarines and ships with Spearfish torpedoes and targets ashore with Tomahawk cruise missiles.

TRIUMPH was scheduled to end her career in 2022, but in late 2022 she completed a large refit at Devonport Dockyard that will see her life extended out to 2024/25

CROWN COPYRIGHT/MOD

Project MANTA

EXTRA LARGE AUTONOMOUS UNDERWATER VEHICLE (XL-AUV)

Name	Pennant Number	Completion Date	Builder
MANTA	S201	2021	MSubs

Displacement: 17 tonnes **Dimensions:** 12m x 2.2m **Machinery:** Electric propulsion with diesel generators **Speed:** 5 knots **Armament:** None **Range:** 1,000 nautical miles

Notes: MANTA is the largest unmanned and most complex underwater system yet operated by the Royal Navy or any European navy. The contract for its construction was awarded in late 2022 to the Plymouth-based tech firm MSubs. She is designed to demonstrate the type for use in the surveillance, reconnaissance and protection of Britain's extensive network of undersea lines of communication such as pipelines, fibre optic cables and similarly vital underwater structures.

MANTA is used by the Royal Navy although ownership of the vessel is retained by MSubs. In October 2023 MANTA conducted a series of what became known as 'D-Day demonstration' runs off a Cornish beach, reminscent of the 1944 operations by mini-subs in preparation of the D-Day landings in World War Two. The results of MANTA's simulated operations were satellite linked to one of the Royal Navy's containerised Portable Operation Centre's (POCs), which conceivably could be located anywhere globally, onboard ships or even ashore.

Upon completion of the trials in 2027 and construction of a larger vessel under Project CETUS, MANTA will be returned to her owners for possible onward sale. MSubs is currently building a second vessel of similar characteristics to MANTA at a cost of £21.5 million and is expected to commence a six-year trials programme from the end of 2024.

CROWN COPYRIGHT/MOD

PROJECT CETUS

Notes: Project CETUS - named after a mythological sea creature - is designed to use the information and operational evaluations obtained through MANTA to further define the characteristics required of a submersible vessel designed to protect underwater installations. CETUS is the first logical step in developing an independent operational autonomous submarine that can be utilised alongside existing submarines such as the Astutes and their successors, or crucially independently. Another aspect of the vehicle being crewless is that the submarine can operate at considerably deeper depths than a comparable manned submarine.

The submersible is reconfigurable to match mission requirements with a payload bay that can be additionally extended by adding another section, doubling the capacity. The main aim of the project is to evaluate how such XL-AUVs could complement the future replacement Astute-class SSN. Project CETUS is being developed under the terms of the Royal Navy's Project SPEARHEAD designed to increase the Royal Navy's mass in underwater warfighting capabilities. It is expected that the number of large unmanned underwater vehicles will increase rapidly towards the year 2040.

Currently there are numerous strands of potential development being evaluated under CETUS (Annex H), CHARYBDIS (Annex F) and the overarching development of a system for enhanced anti-submarine warfare. All these strands are feeding information and data towards the development of a definitive XLUUV for the Royal Navy. It is widely expected that the next Integrated Defence Review, expected in 2025, will make clear the future course of travel in the development of such vessels. What is already known is that this type of submersible can dive deeper and have enhanced endurance over the present generation under evaluation. Modular design will make the substitution of mission specific payloads easier to interchange into the Main Payload Space (MPS) which is 2m x 2m x 2m. The design also provides for additional, although smaller, payload spaces fore and aft.

● L3 HARRIS   Iver4 580 AUV

PROJECT HECLA: AUTONOMOUS UNDERWATER VEHICLES

Notes: In 2023 the UK Government awarded contracts worth £6 million for the development and delivery of two 1,000m depth diving capable Gavia Offshore Surveyor AUVs (made by Teledyne Marine) and a trio of IVER4 580 AUVs (made by L3 Harris). These vehicles will be used for a variety of military tasks including, but not exclusively, to survey, multi-domain intelligence gathering, surveillance and reconnaissance missions and even anti-submarine and mine warfare applications.

These autonomous drones will in future supplant conventional surface ships as the drones are much more portable featuring a modular design with interchangeable components that can be tailored to specific tasks. Each is equipped with a variety of sensor packages including side-scan sonar, multi-beam echo sounders and acoustic doppler current profilers.

The Gavia AUV is capable of delivering high quality data while operating from vessels or from the shore. The Gavia AUV's ease of use and versatility can serve a multitude of purposes without sacrificing performance or data quality. The Iver4 580 offers users a 300-metre depth survey system featuring hot-swappable battery sections that can be changed in the field without any special tools. It is the second vehicle in the Iver4 family of next-generation AUVs to address a wide variety of customer missions, including surveillance and reconnaissance (ISR), anti-submarine warfare (ASW), seabed warfare and mine warfare.

These machines are being acquired under the terms of Project HECLA specially designed to optimise the Royal Navy's future ability to collect and exploit hydrographic information in an efficient, cost effective and timely manner. These new and innovative systems, while replacing surface ships, offer a wider range of possibilities to explore and chart previously inaccessible parts of the world's oceans. For the Royal Navy the North Atlantic seabed is of critical importance particularly for submarine operations.

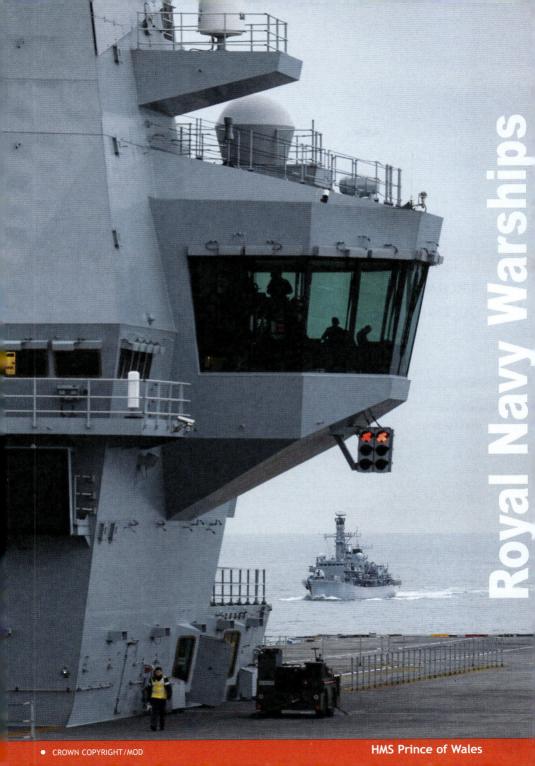

Royal Navy Warships

CROWN COPYRIGHT/MOD

HMS Prince of Wales

CROWN COPYRIGHT/MOD   HMS Queen Elizabeth

AIRCRAFT CARRIER
QUEEN ELIZABETH CLASS

Ship	Pennant Number	Completion Date	Builder
QUEEN ELIZABETH	R08	2017	Aircraft Carrier Alliance
PRINCE OF WALES	R09	2019	Aircraft Carrier Alliance

Displacement: 65,500 tonnes FL **Dimensions:** 282.9m x 38.8m x 11m **Machinery:** Integrated Full Electric Propulsion; 2 RR MT30 GT alternators, 93,870 hp (70 MW), 4 Wärtsilä DG, 53,064 hp (39.6 MW); 4 induction motors, 53,640 hp (40 MW); 2 shafts **Speed:** 26 knots **Armament:** 3 x Phalanx, 4 x 30mm **Aircraft:** Up to 36 x F-35B Lightning and 4 x Merlin ASaC (Crowsnest). Typical mix could be 12-24 F-35B and various helicopters which could include Merlin, Chinook, Wildcat and Apache **Complement:** 686 + 830 Air Group

Notes: These 65,000 tonnes aircraft carriers are the largest and most complex surface vessels ever designed, built, and operated by the Royal Navy. Each ship can accommodate all military helicopter types currently in the British armed forces (Navy, Army and Air Force) plus up to 40 F-35B Lightning II Joint Strike Fighters.

Since December 2020, the United Kingdom has had a Carrier Strike capability resting in these two ships. The two ships have, over the last couple of years, had very different careers, while QUEEN ELIZABETH has successfully, for the most part, expanded the operating capabilities of the Class by deploying a wide variety of British and Allied aircraft, notably the American V-22 Osprey tilt rotor aircraft, her sister ship PRINCE OF WALES has languished at Rosyth undergoing extremely expensive, time consuming and publicly embarrassing repairs to her propulsion and steering. While at Rosyth the MoD has taken the opportunity to upgrade the ship in several important aspects, making her the most sophisticated warship in the Royal Navy's fleet. She completed the repairs in August 2023 and returned to Portsmouth.

The two ships will in 2024 provide the Royal Navy with a carrier strike capability not seen since the days of HMS ARK ROYAL and HMS EAGLE in the late 1960s. 2024 was going to be a busy one for both ships with QUEEN ELIZABETH taking part in EXERCISE STEADFAST DEFENDER while PRINCE OF WALES was scheduled to deploy to the United States for her much delayed WESTLANT deployment to fully integrate the F-35B Lightning II Joint Strike fighter into the ship together with trials of unmanned aerial vehicles and American aircraft types such as the V-22 Osprey. On completion she will be ready for her 2025 UK Carrier Strike Group global deployment, probably to the Far East.

But at the beginning of February warships from NATO countries were preparing to take part in EXERCISE STEADFAST DEFENDER 2024 - the largest NATO exercise in Europe, involving more than 40 vessels from 31 allied nations, since the Cold War. One of Britain's two state-of-the-art aircraft carriers - HMS QUEEN ELIZABETH - was scheduled to take part in the exercise but had to pull out after an issue with "a coupling on the starboard propellor shaft" was found during routine pre-sailing checks. Perhaps something similar to the issue HMS PRINCE OF WALES encountered 2 years ago to her propeller shaft when she was about to sail for training exercises with the United States and Canada off the East coast of North America which resulted in her being 'out of action' for almost a year. Within seven days she was replaced by sister ship PRINCE OF WALES. Such a quick turnaround (the scaffolding on her deck had to be taken down, crew had to be gathered, ammunition had to be loaded aboard, etc.) was hailed as a success by the Royal Navy, whilst the Financial Times reported that the last-minute change of plan was "highly embarrassing" and would "compound concerns over limitations to the Royal Navy's capabilities".

• CROWN COPYRIGHT/MOD — HMS Prince of Wales

CROWN COPYRIGHT/MOD

HMS Prince of Wales

On 24 July 2023, HMS PRINCE OF WALES, Britain's biggest warship, sailed from Rosyth, Scotland. After nine months undergoing engineering repairs and receiving significant capability enhancements to support her future tasking, she moved out of dry dock at Rosyth and into the River Forth. Once at anchor and in deeper water, the ship's team will prove machinery and bring her systems to life – before sailing under the iconic Forth Bridges on her way to Portsmouth.

She deployed from Portsmouth on 5 September 2023 for flying trials on the US East Coast, including working with F35Bs, V22 Osprey Martins and General Atomics MQIC remotely piloted UAS. Towards the end of February 2024, a national newspaper reported that Chancellor Jeremy Hunt was planning to cut defence spending in the next Budget, especially because - as reported in *Warship World* - the government and the treasury do not believe the MoD will manage its finances sufficiently and therefore are reluctant to increase defence spending. The alternative to balance the Defence books if the Budget will not include any (significant) rise in defence spending was, and perhaps the worst one to be proposed, but discussed by members of the Maritime Enterprise Planning Group, which looks at future considerations and strategies, is to mothball HMS PRINCE OF WALES, which cost £3.5 billion to build, or even worse, sold for a knockdown price to a friendly nation, over the fleet's flagship HMS QUEEN ELIZABETH. Such a move would probably be divisive, however the decision could be forced upon commanders as soon as 2028 if the state-of-defence finances does not improve. The MEP group is aware that the Navy is struggling to maintain operational commitments and has to expand the fleet as rapidly as possible. Therefore, the second carrier is an asset that is held in reserve and is a very expensive piece of rarely-used equipment. So their thoughts are that if they need to address balance sheet issues, disposing of her or sharing her with an AUKUS member, would be an option. It is no secret that financial consequences wasn't the only reason the UK turned down an excellent opportunity to send an aircraft carrier to the Red Sea, as it is widely accepted that the UK will not be able to adequately defend or operate the aircraft carrier independently. The aircraft carrier and strike group have previously relied on protection from (NATO) allies including the Netherlands and the US.

● GORDON BRODIE   HMS Albion

LANDING PLATFORM DOCK
ALBION CLASS

Ship	Pennant Number	Completion Date	Builder
ALBION	L14	2003	BAE Systems
BULWARK	L15	2004	BAE Systems

Displacement: 18,797 tonnes FL, 21,500 tonnes (flooded) **Dimensions** 176m x 28.9m x 7.1m
Machinery: Diesel-electric; 2 Wärtsilä Vasa 32E DG, 17,000 hp (12.5 MW); 2 Wärtsilä Vasa 32LNE DG, 4,216 hp (3.1 MW); 2 motors; 2 shafts; 1 bow thruster **Speed:** 18 knots
Armament: 2 x CIWS, 2 x 20mm guns (single) **Complement:** 325 Military Lift 303 troops, with an overload capacity of a further 405

Notes: These highly versatile vessels provide the Royal Navy with its amphibious punch and were designed with the function of landing Royal Marines ashore by air and by sea. They also have extensive command and control facilities and can operate as flagships for operations and major deployments.

Each ship has deck capacity for up to six Army Challenger main battle tanks or around 30 armoured all-terrain vehicles. A floodable well dock aft can accommodate four LCU Mk10 utility landing craft, while four smaller LCVP Mk5B landing craft are carried on davits.

ALBION and BULWARK have a large flight deck capable of receiving all British and most Allied helicopter types currently in service but neither have hangar facilities. The flight deck is arranged with two landing spots for simultaneous operation of two RAF Chinook helicopters.

It is Royal Navy policy to have one of these vessels operational while the other is retained in reserve or refit. In 2017 ALBION re-emerged having been laid up since 2012 and assumed the role of Fleet Flagship, subsequently passed onto HMS QUEEN ELIZABETH in 2020.

ALBION continued in service until July 2023 when she was de-stored at Plymouth and prepared for reserve. Her sistership BULWARK nominally replaced her in the operational fleet although for a while there were no operational assault ships in the Royal Navy in 2023. It is expected that ALBION will be in reserve for another five years before being refitted for further service for what is expected to be her last commission between 2028-2033. ALBION and BULWARK's out of service dates are 2033 and 2034 respectively.

In 2022 Defence Procurement Minister Jeremy Quinn MP stated in a written reply to another MP that plans for a replacement are now underway with the design at *"concept stage"*. These may include purchasing an off-the-shelf European design of LPD to speed up the delivery of this enormously useful and versatile capability.

In July 2023 the UK and Dutch governments issued a joint statement stating their aims to design and develop a joint future assault ship for their respective fleets. The Royal Navy's two Albion-class ships ALBION and BULWARK are due to be retired from service in the early 2030s and the Royal Netherlands Navy have a similar issue with their two assault ships ROTTERDAM and JOHAN DE WITT. For the Royal Navy these new vessels come under the auspices of the Future UK Multi Role Support Ship (MRSS) programme and according to UK Defence Minister James Cartlidge and his Dutch counterpart Kajse Ollongren the ships will "be equipped with a sea-to-land strike capability, designed to operate in amphibious task groups – known as Littoral Response Groups – helping highly-trained Marines to deploy to crises globally, fully equipped with their vehicles, boats, aircraft, and weaponry."

Despite these positive moves there are persistent rumours that ALBION may be sold with Brazil being touted as a likely purchaser. If this is proved to be correct such a sale, before replacements have been procured, would seriously erode the Royal Marines effectiveness and the nations amphibious capability would be reduced to barely adequate.

- CROWN COPYRIGHT/MOD HMS Albion

British Warships & Auxiliaries 2024

• CROWN COPYRIGHT/MOD　　　　　　　　　　　　　　　　HMS Duncan

DESTROYERS
DARING CLASS (Type 45)

Ship	Pennant Number	Completion Date	Builder
DARING	D32	2008	BVT Surface Fleet
DAUNTLESS	D33	2008	BVT Surface Fleet
DIAMOND	D34	2009	BVT Surface Fleet
DRAGON	D35	2011	BVT Surface Fleet
DEFENDER	D36	2012	BVT Surface Fleet
DUNCAN	D37	2013	BVT Surface Fleet

Displacement: 7,350 tonnes **Dimensions:** 152.4m x 21.2m x 5.7m **Machinery:** Integrated Electric Propulsion; 2 RR WR-21 GT alternators, 67,600 hp (49.7 MW); 2 Wärtsilä DG (4 MW); 2 Converteam motors (40 MW); 2 shafts **Speed:** 29 knots **Armament:** 1 - 4.5-inch gun, 2 x Quad Harpoon missile launchers (on four ships), Sea Viper missile system comprising Sylver VLS with combination of up to 48 Aster 15 and Aster 30 missiles, 2 x Vulcan Phalanx (fitted as required) **Aircraft:** Wildcat or Merlin **Complement:** 190 (with space for 235)

Notes: These six vessels were originally planned to replace the preceding Type 42 destroyers on a ship-for-ship basis but the original plan to buy twelve (down from 14 Type 42s) was cut to 8 and then finally six in June 2008 with all these ships entering service by 2013.

Central to the success of the design is its 18,000mph Sea Viper anti-aircraft missile system which can knock-out enemy targets at ranges up to 70 miles from the ship. This potent weapon is linked to the powerful Sampson Multi-Function Radar that can track hundreds of targets at previously unheard distances. The latest version of the S1850M long range radar can track up to 1,000 air targets at around 400 kilometres in 3D.

It was claimed at the time of their inception that with these key systems the six destroyers could cover more surface area than a comparable Type 42 and thus fewer hulls were required. Or could it have been the £1 billion price tag for each of the new warships?

Since their first acceptance into service, the Type 45 destroyers received criticism over the perceived weakness of their propulsion plants. They use a pioneering Integrated Electric Propulsion (IEP) system – the first time that it has been used in a major warship design. The system comprises GE alternators driven by two Rolls-Royce WR-21 gas turbines, with two Wärtsilä 12V200 diesel generators providing electrical power at 4,160V to a GE high voltage system. The high voltage system is then used to provide power to the two GE Power Conversion advanced motors with outputs of 20MW each.

As long ago as 2016 the Government admitted that the Northrop Grumman intercooler was unreliable and prone to breaking down, particularly in hot and dry conditions. The solution was settled upon with a March 2018 announcement stating that Cammell Laird shipyard in Birkenhead would undertake restorative refits on all six ships by replacing their faulty diesel engines with three new ones, therefore adding another layer of redundancy into the system. This series of initiatives was christened 'The Power Improvement Project for the Type 45'. The programme of rectification and upgrading of these ships is almost complete.

On May 24, 2022, the Ministry of Defence announced that the Type 45 destroyers will be refitted with upgraded sensors and weaponry to intercept and destroy ballistic missiles. The Ballistic Missile Defence Capability (BMD) will be a major milestone in the history of the class as they will become the first European warships to field this capability, that up till now was the preserve of the United States, Russia and Japan. The Aster 30 Block 1NT (New Technology) missile has been developed for the land-based SAMP-T Ballistic missile defence system and has been adapted for naval use through the Sylver VLS and offering a range of some 600 kilometres. The need for greater accuracy and range has been met with the Aster 30 Block 1NT missiles being fitted with a new Ka-band radar seeker head. Future developments of the Aster Block 2 missile are said to be continuing with advertised ranges out to 3,000 kilometres. Existing Royal Navy stockpiles of Aster missiles will be upgraded to Block 1 standard and will differ slightly from their French and Italian counterparts.

BMD is part of an ongoing programme of incremental improvements to the Type 45 destroyers that also includes the Sea Viper Evolution programme (SV-E) that have seen significant upgrades made to the six Type 45 destroyer's Sampson multi-function radar (MFR). It is also expected that the current capacity of 48 missiles carried by each Type 45 destroyer will be increased to 72 between 2026 and 2032.

CROWN COPYRIGHT/MOD   HMS Richmond

FRIGATES
TYPE 23 (ASW Variant)

Ship	Pennant Number	Completion Date	Builder
KENT	F78	2000	Yarrow
PORTLAND	F79	2000	Yarrow
SUTHERLAND	F81	1997	Yarrow
SOMERSET	F82	1996	Yarrow
ST ALBANS	F83	2001	Yarrow
WESTMINSTER	F237	1993	Swan Hunter
NORTHUMBERLAND	F238	1994	Swan Hunter
RICHMOND	F239	1994	Swan Hunter

Displacement: 4,900 tonnes **Dimensions:** 133m x 16.1m x 5.5m **Machinery:** CODLAG; 2 RR Spey GT, 31,100 hp (23.2 MW); 4 Paxman diesels 8,100 hp (6 MW); 2 GEC motors, 4,000 hp (3 MW); 2 shafts **Speed:** 28 knots **Armament:** Harpoon or Sea Ceptor; 1 x 4.5-inch gun, 2 x single 30mm guns, 2 x twin (324 mm) Sting Ray Torpedo Tubes **Aircraft:** Wildcat or Merlin helicopter **Complement:** 185

Notes: The Type 23 provide the backbone to the Royal Navy's surface fleet and, whilst primarily designed for the anti-submarine warfare conditions found at the end of the Cold War, have proven to be capable general-purpose vessels in the new technologically dominated battlespace. When originally conceived in the early 1980s the Type 23 was to

British Warships & Auxiliaries 2024

have been a relatively limited, affordable escort, but following the lessons of the Falklands War of 1982 the design was recast and grew out of all recognition to the first straightforward design concepts. With this extra growth came a parallel increase in the cost of acquisition of new ships and, while the original ships had an expected service life of little more than twelve years, they have been modernised and patched up, but with even the youngest of the Type 23 frigates approaching 24 years of age, they are falling apart.

The Royal Navy's ambition is to keep these relatively old vessels at the forefront of technology and to bridge the gap between the first of the class leaving service and the introduction into service of the first of the new Type 26 City-class frigates from around 2025. To achieve this the ships have received a LIFEX (Life Extension) programme of retrofits. This capability sustainment includes, but is not limited to, the removal of the legacy Seawolf anti-aircraft missile and its replacement with the more modern and capable Seaceptor missiles, extensive hull maintenance and weapon and sensor upgrades to allow the ships to keep pace with the latest military developments around the globe.

The Type 23 Life Extension programme has not been a straightforward programme to manage especially on costs. Each frigate refit has its own unique problems to identify, source a solution and to correct. No two refits have enjoyed a similar timeframe with HMS ST ALBANS's current refit already stretching out beyond 40 months and HMS IRON DUKE's refit lasting 53 months. Her refit was widely reported as being the most complex and challenging so far faced by the Royal Navy and that led to expensive cost overruns. At a time of limited repair budgets and changing priorities for the Royal Navy towards autonomous vessels, artificial intelligence and machine learning, expensive legacy assets could possibly be seen as a worthwhile sacrificial lamb to the slaughter to save money.

• LEO MARRIOTT   HMS Richmond

However, on the other hand, the Type 23s are the Royal Navy's primary and most potent anti-submarine warfare units, especially those equipped with the Type 2087 Towed Array sonar, including HMS WESTMINSTER. The unit could potentially be removed and retrofitted to another hull (either ARGYLL or IRON DUKE), but not without a great deal of time, effort and money, and crucially further reducing the available number of frigates to counter the rapidly increasing submarine threat. The Type 2087 sonar could also be fitted to the new Type 26 frigates, the first of which is still at least three years away from entering service, by which time she will have been in build for the laughable long time of around 10 years.

Despite the fact that the Type 23 frigates are creaking under the strain of too many commitments, block obsolescence, under funding and purely being old, they soldier on, except they can't as the recent suspension of HMS WESTMINSTER's latest refit attests to. The refit was halted at Devonport following the discovery of a lengthy list of costly extra requirements to rectify fundamental problems with the structure of the warship, which first launched in 1992.

WESTMINSTER's Life Extension refit was completed in 2017 and five years later she was taken in hand at Devonport in October 2022 for another refit to extend her service to 2028. Engineers found that she was in such a bad material state that her refit would be throwing good money after bad. It is unlikely that she will go to sea again and she will probably soon go to the shipbreakers, sooner than expected leaving a hole in the already anorexic thin line of frigates and destroyers. With just five Type 23s available for tasking (including HMS LANCASTER based out in the Persian Gulf), this leaves precious little in the bank for emergencies.

Crucial to the LIFEX programme is work on the ship's Power Generation Machinery Upgrade (PGMU) which involves the replacement of four main propulsion diesel generator sets. So far only HMS ST ALBANS has completed the integration of the new power units. Another, less well publicised aspect of the refit is the installation of new 'stealth' technologies designed to assist in the detection of enemy deep-submerged submarines and furthermore means to defend the frigates from detection themselves by the very submarines they are tracking. Work on the Type 23s has all been carried out at Babcock's Devonport Dockyard where over 1,000 people work on the programme.

Over the next five years the remaining Type 23 frigates will receive technical upgrades to their magazine torpedo launch systems and threat countermeasures capabilities. The upgrades will be conducted by Systems Engineering & Assessment (SEA). These upgrades will also include advancements for SEAGNAT decoy deployers. (These will also be fitted to Type 45 destroyers and RFA tankers).

The planned (provisional) decommissioning dates are: WESTMINSTER (2024 moved from 2028); NORTHUMBERLAND (2029); RICHMOND (2030); SOMERSET (2031); SUTHERLAND (2032); KENT (2033); PORTLAND (2034) and ST ALBANS (2035).

CROWN COPYRIGHT/MOD · HMS Lancaster

FRIGATES
TYPE 23 (GP Variant)

Ship	Pennant Number	Completion Date	Builder
LANCASTER	F229	1991	Yarrow
ARGYLL	F231	1991	Yarrow
IRON DUKE	F234	1992	Yarrow

Displacement: 4,900 tonnes **Dimensions:** 133m x 16.1m x 5.5m **Machinery:** CODLAG; 2 RR Spey GT, 31,100 hp (23.2 MW); 4 Paxman diesels 8,100 hp (6 MW); 2 GEC motors, 4,000 hp (3 MW); 2 shafts **Speed:** 28 knots **Armament:** Harpoon or Sea Ceptor; 1 - 4.5-inch gun, 2 x single 30mm guns, 2 x twin (324 mm) Sting Ray Torpedo Tubes **Aircraft:** Wildcat or Merlin helicopter **Complement:** 185

Notes: These ships have not been retrofitted with the advanced Type 2037 sonar system and operate in the General-Purpose role. As these ships are the oldest Type 23s in the fleet it is expected that they will be the first to be replaced by the new Type 31 frigates when they enter service. In 2019 IRON DUKE was towed to Plymouth for her LIFEX refit that was expected to see her fitted with a new 3D Artisan radar and air defence weapon system and Sea Ceptor missiles replacing her legacy Seawolf. This refit, which included significant structural work, was twice as long as any previous Duke-class frigate, clocking-up a staggering 1.7 million man-hours of labour in the longest LIFEX programme yet undertaken on the Type-23 frigate. MONTROSE was withdrawn from service in 2023. The out of service dates for the remaining three ships remain LANCASTER (2024), IRON DUKE (2025) and ARGYLL (2026/2027).

- BAE SYSTEMS

FRIGATES
CITY CLASS (Type 26)

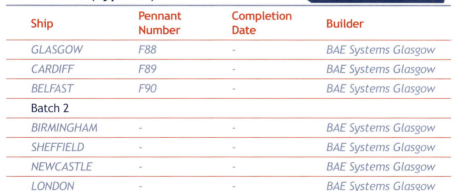

Ship	Pennant Number	Completion Date	Builder
GLASGOW	F88	-	BAE Systems Glasgow
CARDIFF	F89	-	BAE Systems Glasgow
BELFAST	F90	-	BAE Systems Glasgow
Batch 2			
BIRMINGHAM	-	-	BAE Systems Glasgow
SHEFFIELD	-	-	BAE Systems Glasgow
NEWCASTLE	-	-	BAE Systems Glasgow
LONDON	-	-	BAE Systems Glasgow
EDINBURGH	-	-	BAE Systems Glasgow

Displacement: 8,000+ tonnes full load **Dimensions:** 149.9m x 20.8m **Machinery:** CODLOG; 2 shafts **Speed:** 26+ knots **Range:** 7,000 nautical miles **Armament:** 12-cell VLS for 48 Sea Ceptor anti-air missiles, 24-cell Mk 41 VLS for Tomahawk, 1 x 5 inch 62 calibre Mk 45 naval gun, 2 x 30mm DS30M Mk2 guns, 2 x Phalanx CIWS, 2 x miniguns, 4 x general purpose machine guns **Aircraft:** up to two helicopters (Wildcat) armed with 4 x anti-ship missiles, or 2 anti-submarine torpedoes, 20 Martlet multi-role air-to-surface missiles and Mk 11 depth charges or 1 x Merlin armed with 4 anti-submarine torpedoes **Complement:** 157 (capacity for 208)

Notes: The long-drawn-out timeframe associated with the design and development of modern warships is plain to see in the development of the Type 26 or City-class frigates.

Planning for the replacement of the Type 22 and Type 23 frigates of the surface fleet started in 1998 with the commencement of the Future Surface Combatant (FSC) programme. The research trimaran RV TRITON was procured but in the end more conventional hull designs were chosen over radical innovations. In March 2005, two versions of the FSC were announced showing a two-class series of ships, one 'Medium Sized Vessel Derivative' for service in the 2016-19 timeframe and a more capable 'Versatile Surface Combatant' entering service from around 2023.

Defence officials, trying to get the best bang for their buck circa 2006, explored the possibilities of extracting the maximum synergies between the FSC and the need for replacement survey ships and minesweepers under the Sustained Surface Combatant Capability (S2C2) programme. There were three clear requirements for the Royal Navy at this time: C1 - a high-end anti-submarine dedicated vessel of around 6,000 tonnes displacement; C2 - a general-purpose platform of around 4-5,000 tonnes and C3, a Global Corvette which could replace most of the survey and mine warfare fleet in service.

In 2008 the FSC concept was brought forward in the budget at the expense of building another pair of Type 45 destroyers. Detailed design work on the new C1 and C2 concepts was handed over to BAE Systems in 2009. Each vessel would have an expected lifespan of 25 years with one being built every year for a total of 18 (10C1 and 8C2 variants).

Crucially the first of the FSCs were to have entered service in 2020. In 2020 the mine warfare aspect of the programme was dropped in favour of the Mine Countermeasures, Hydrography and Patrol Capability (MHPC) programme. In 2010 FSC became the Global Combat Ship and expectations were high that the first of class might be in service by 2021.

2010, however, was the year of the 2010 Strategic Defence and Security Review that stripped the Royal Navy of the highly capable Type 22 frigates and ARK ROYAL, and the Harrier jump jets. Orders for new ships were farmed off into the long grass for a while and the programme started to slip. The Government's decision to reduce the size of the surface fleet to just 19 escorts also meant that there would be fewer orders for the Global Combat Ship. The Government also insisted that the specifications for the Global Combat Ship be pared down on a cost saving exercise from around £500m per ship to around £250m - £350m per vessel. However, this decision was later recinded and in February 2015 BAE Systems signed a £859m MoD contract to continue development and work towards manufacture. Ultimately, on 2 July 2017 BAE Systems was awarded a £3.7 billion contract for the first three ships at their Govan shipyard on the Clyde.

In design, the Global Combat Ship has modularity and flexibility as key capability enhancers to allow the ships to operate in as wide a range of scenarios as possible, from full-scale war to maritime security, counter piracy or humanitarian relief. Through life support offered by BAE Systems is another key component in ensuring that the hulls remain relevant throughout the next three decades as technology develops and can be replaced relatively easily. The Royal Navy Type 26 ships will be equipped with the Type 997 Artisan 3D search radar and the Sea Ceptor (CAMM) anti-air-defence missile system launched via 48 vertical launch system (VLS) canisters. An additional 24-cell Mk 41 'strike length VLS' cells are positioned forward of the bridge and can accommodate long-range strike weapons such as Tomahawk land-attack cruise missiles and future long-range supersonic anti-ship and anti-land weapons.

The City Class's primary role remains that of anti-submarine warfare and for this the ship's hulls have been designed to be acoustically quiet. They are equipped with powerful Ultra Electronics Type 2150 next generation bow mounted sonar and a Sonar 2087 towed array. Each ship will be up-gunned from the current 4.5 inch calibre gun of the Type 23s and Type 45s to mount a NATO standard BAE 5inch, 62 calibre Mk 45 naval gun. For propulsion, the Type 26s will feature a gas turbine direct drive and four high speed diesel generators driving a pair of electric motors in a combined diesel-electric or gas (CODLOG) configuration.

In 2023 it was announced that the Type 26 frigates will be equipped with a new advanced weapons handling system developed by BAE Systems Inc. The company received a contract to fit five Mk 45 Maritime Indirect Fire Systems (MIFS). MIFS combines the 5-inch 62 calibre Mk45 Mod 4A naval gun with its associated automated ammunition handling system (AHS). The system is being introduced on Royal Navy warships and will provide an enhanced level of compatibility with similarly equipped American warships. The MIFS systems will be manufactured at BAE Systems Minneapolis and Louisville Kentucky facilities.

The first-of-class was named GLASGOW, with steel being cut in her construction on 20 July 2017. By late 2021 the first three members of the class were in various stages of construction. GLASGOW is expected to be commissioned in 2028 which will mean that she took more than a decade to build and commission into service! In mid-November 2022 the £4.2 billion order for the five ships of Batch 2 was confirmed by the UK Government with the first Batch 2 vessel BIRMINGHAM being laid down on 4 April 2023.

The Type 26 design has been chosen by Canada and Australia as the basis for their frigate replacement programmes, respectively the Canadian Surface Combatant and the Hunter Class. Canada is building up to 15 ships and Australia nine. Both nations are procuring many more hulls than the Royal Navy.

• CROWN COPYRIGHT/MOD — Future HMS Glasgow (in December 2022)

• BABCOCK INTERNATIONAL   Future HMS Venturer

FRIGATES
INSPIRATION CLASS (Type 31)

Ship	Pennant Number	Completion Date	Builder
VENTURER	-	Building	Babcock International
BULLDOG	-	Ordered	Babcock International
CAMPBELTOWN	-	Ordered	Babcock International
FORMIDABLE	-	Ordered	Babcock International
ACTIVE	-	Building	Babcock International

Displacement: 5,700 tonnes **Dimensions:** 138.7m x 19.8m x 5m **Machinery:** 4 x Rolls Royce/MTU 20V 8000 M71 diesel engines, 4 x Rolls Royce/MTU 16V 2000 M41B generators = 32+ MW electric propulsion system **Speed:** 28+ knots **Range:** 9,000 nautical miles **Armament:** Bofors 57mm Mk 3 naval gun, 2 x 40mm guns, 4 x 7.62 machine guns, 4 x 7.62mm mini guns, up to 24 cell Sea Ceptor anti-aircraft missiles **Aircraft:** Either a single AugustaWestland Wildcat HMA2 or AugustaWestland Merlin Mk 2 helicopter **Complement:** 80-100 (accommodation for up to 160)

Notes: Construction of the first components for VENTURER commenced on 23 September 2021 in the specially built £31.5 million state-of-the-art 147-metre long and 30-metre high construction hall at Rosyth Dockyard. The official laying of her keel took place on 26th April 2022. To speed construction, and possibly to reduce costs in the process, two ships of the class can be built simultaneously side by side in this vast building. The class evolved from the 2010 Strategic Defence and Security Review and emerging from the Global Combat Ship these future vessels will complement the Type 32 frigate and the more capable Type 26 frigates. They are expected to enter service in the late 2020s. The class is the first to be ordered under the so-called Pathfinder programmes established under the auspices of the National Shipbuilding Programme that aims to create and maintain a steady and healthy drumbeat of warship construction across the United Kingdom rather than the drip feed that has been the norm for near on four decades. Under the Pathfinder programmes shipyards across the country will be able to bid on programmes that will sustain employment and innovative technological progress in shipbuilding whilst updating and modernising the Royal Navy's core escort fleet, which has taken an unprecedented hammering across a succession of defence reviews since the end of World War Two.

The Type 31e has been designed to fit in the capability gap roughly between the Type 26 frigates and those of the River II-class offshore patrol vessels. That being said these frigates will not be Second Rate vessels of old as they will be equipped with the latest technology and weaponry such as a Bofors 57mm Mk 3 naval gun, 40mm guns and the Sea Ceptor anti-air missile system in vertical launch tubes.

The Type 31e is based on Babcock's Arrowhead 140 design and is modular, so it is likely that they may be readily reconfigurable to match specific mission or deployment profiles. These mission bays will be flexible and adaptable at short notice and will allow these vessels to provide a reassuring presence to British Overseas Territories and be capable of worldwide deployment on long-term missions in support of British political, security, military and economic aims.

HMS VENTURER is scheduled to be launched this year but her entry into service will be 2027. Interestingly the names chosen for this class were chosen to reflect five key themes around future Royal Navy missions. The Type 31 design has also been chosen by the Polish Navy as their future frigate design.

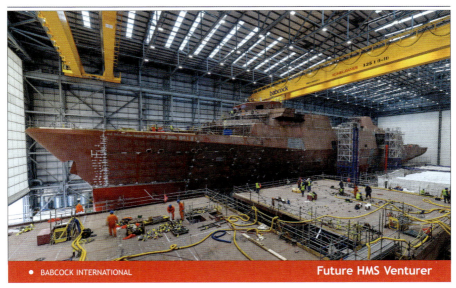

● BABCOCK INTERNATIONAL **Future HMS Venturer**

● DEREK FOX   HMS Brocklesby

MINE COUNTERMEASURES SHIPS (MCMV)
HUNT CLASS

Ship	Pennant Number	Completion Date	Builder
LEDBURY	M30	1981	Vosper T
CATTISTOCK	M31	1982	Vosper T
BROCKLESBY	M33	1983	Vosper T
MIDDLETON	M34	1984	Yarrow
CHIDDINGFOLD	M37	1984	Vosper T
HURWORTH	M39	1985	Vosper T

Displacement: 750 tonnes FL **Dimensions:** 60m x 10.5m x 3.4m **Machinery:** 2 Caterpillar C32 ACERT diesels; 1 Deltic 9-55B diesel for pulse generator and auxiliary drive; 2 shafts; 1 bow thruster **Speed:** 15 knots **Armament:** 1 x 30mm; 2 x Miniguns **Complement:** 45 crew and 5 officers

Notes: With the introduction of new autonomous methods of dealing with the threat posed by sea mines, the future for the mine countermeasures vessels of the Hunt Class would seem on paper to be limited. Under current plans, over the next few years the oldest members of the class will be retired from service and replaced with autonomous systems that can be remotely operated from a wide variety of naval vessels from a safe distance removing the danger to life posed by these weapons.

LEDBURY, the oldest member of the fleet, entered service as long ago as 1980 but regular retrofits have enabled the ship to remain current when faced with an increasingly technologically advanced threat that is becoming more deadly and harder to combat with each successive year. Refits often include improved diesel generators, along with upgraded hull and crew accommodation. During a refit the team at BAE Systems completes over 65,000 production hours on each MCMV including a full structural re-baselining of the ship with over two miles of laminating cloth being laid, extensive system enhancements undertaken, as well as maintenance and defect rectification.

Two members of the class, CHIDDINGFOLD and BROCKLESBY, are forward deployed to the Persian Gulf to provide a permanent Royal Navy presence together with two Sandown-class minehunters as part of Operation Kipion. The four MCMVs use highly trained Mine Clearance Divers and the SeaFox unmanned mine disposal system to detect and neutralise mines.

The Hunt Class will be replaced in service by new autonomous mine-warfare vessels that are cheaper and more expendable than manned vessels. The Royal Navy is collaborating with their French counterparts in the development of a £117 million Maritime Mine Counter Measures (MMCM). It is expected that the last of the Hunt Class will leave service by 2031.

A freak accident occurred in Mina Salman port in Bahrain on 19 January 2024 when the Royal Navy's Hunt-class MCMV HMS CHIDDINGFOLD hit the moored Sandown-class minehunter HMS BANGOR while leaving port after undergoing major work on the vessel's propulsion system, carried out alongside at the naval base. After being assisted off the berth by two local Svitzer tugs in sunny, calm conditions, it seemed that "full ahead" had been called on the two main engines. However, the minehunter went full astern and hit BANGOR with force on her port side, causing considerable damage and a breach in the vessel's GRP hull.

No crew members on either vessel were injured. Unofficial reports from Bahrain suggest that the accident occurred after the wiring of the propulsion control system on CHIDDINGFOLD had been wrongly reconnected. However, the RN would neither confirm nor deny this report. As HMS BANGOR is the last active Sandown-class MCMV, and shortly to decommission, she is unlikely to be repaired as the RN is now deploying autonomous ROV for minehunting work. The Sandown-class vessel is likely to be scrapped in Bahrain (the local ASRY shipyard is certified for such work), or returned to the UK on a heavy transport vessel and scrapped. There is also the possibility that the vessel could be repaired in the UK if an overseas navy is interested in purchasing the ship. If CHIDDINGFOLD needs to be dry-docked and repaired, the ASRY (Arab Shipbuilding & Repair Yard) in Bahrain is more than capable of undertaking this work, as it has worked on a number of RN and RFA vessels in recent years, as well as US Navy vessels.

• CROWN COPYRIGHT/MOD　　　　　　　　　　　　　　　　　　　　　HMS Penzance

MINE COUNTERMEASURES SHIPS
SANDOWN CLASS

Ship	Pennant Number	Completion Date	Builder
PENZANCE	M106	1998	Vosper T
BANGOR	M109	2000	Vosper T

Displacement: 600 tonnes **Dimensions:** 52.5m x 10.9m x 2.3m **Machinery:** 2 Paxman Valenta diesels, 1,523 hp; Voith-Schneider propulsion; 2 bow thrusters **Speed:** 13 knots **Armament:** 1 x 30mm gun; 2 x Miniguns; 3 x GPMG **Complement:** 34

Notes: The Sandown-class Mine Counter Measure Vessels are based in Scotland. The staff and ships of Mine Counter Measures 1 (MCM1) Squadron deploy in the Northern Gulf, conduct NATO exercises with other nations and work around the British Coastline, protecting the United Kingdom's shores and clearing the old ordnance that remains as a legacy of previous wars.

The two surviving Sandown-class vessels are to be gradually replaced in service by new unmanned autonomous mine disposal systems by 2025. The Sandown Class will be retired before the more capable Hunt-class vessels. These ships are still comparatively young, and it is very likely that they will be sold abroad for further service.

PEMBROKE and her already decommissioned sister ship BLYTH were sold in late 2023 to Romania. PEMBROKE will leave Royal Navy service early in 2024. On 9 January 2024, HMS PENZANCE held a ceremony alongside HMNB Clyde to commemorate the ship sailing from the submarine base for the final time, prior to her formal decommissioning in Rosyth.

● CROWN COPYRIGHT/MOD HMS Lancaster

• DEREK FOX

MINE HUNTING DRONE (MMCM)

Displacement: N/A **Dimensions:** N/A **Payload:** N/A **Speed:** N/A **Complement:** cabin for crew but usually unmanned

Notes: The first drone was handed over to the Royal Navy for evaluation and trials in late 2021 under a Franco British project known in France as SLAM-F and in the United Kingdom as MMCM. The agreement between the two countries was agreed as part of the Lancaster House military agreement (2010). France and Great Britain and to a lesser extent the likes of the Netherlands and Belgium have a very similar geographical requirement for replacement minesweeping and mine-hunting capabilities and also share the same problem of rapidly ageing fleets of legacy mine-warfare vessels. The contract for the design and development of a single drone for both France and Britain was ratified in 2015 with Thales and OCCAR on behalf of the two countries.

The MMCM system comprises two USVs (one of which is fitted with a towed sonar) and the other a remotely operated robot (ROV), and two UAVs. These systems together are tasked with the detection of, classifying of and locating of sea mines in coastal and littoral waters. The ROV will be used to neutralise the threat posed by the mines. Crucial to MMCM is the elimination, as much as possible, of humans in the area of greatest danger. Furthermore, with the use of robotics it will be possible to dive deeper, up to 300 metres, and destroy more weapons more efficiently. The demonstrator was officially handed over to the Royal Navy in Plymouth on 23 November 2021 by staff from Thales UK, OCCAR and Defence Equipment and Support (DE&S), the procurement arm of the UK Ministry of Defence. The three vessels have been given the names ARTEMIS, APOLLO and ABDIEL. In December 2022 APOLLO took part in a joint Anglo-French MMCM programme that saw the vessel operate independently in open water for the first time. These vessels achieve this by using a complicated set of sensors including radar, LIDAR (light detection and ranging), electro-optical and infra-red camera. By linking these sensors together through Thales' MCube mission management software the boats can effectively control themselves and act together or independently.

CROWN COPYRIGHT/MOD

MARITIME MINE COUNTERMEASURES SYSTEMS (MMCS)

Displacement: 6,000 kg **Dimensions:** 11m x 3.2m x 0.5m **Payload:** 4 tonnes **Speed:** 40+ knots
Complement: cabin for crew but usually unmanned

Notes: On 20 January 2021, the MoD awarded Atlas Elektronik UK a £25 million contract to deliver Great Britain's first MHC Block 1 unmanned minesweeper. Two further vessels have been delivered against the contract that utilises autonomous, more expendable vessels against the deadly threat posed by sea mines. HEBE, named after the ancient Greek goddess of youth, joined sister vessels HARRIER and HAZARD as part of the Royal Navy's crewless mine-hunting programme Project Wilton. HEBE has an extended cabin with more technology on board and is four metres longer than her sisters.

The vessels use a system of cutting-edge technologies known as a 'Combined Influence Sweep' which has been developed to combat modern digital sea mines that are more sophisticated than their pressure, acoustic and contact system predecessors. The uncrewed boats will tow innovative Coiled Auxiliary Boats (CABs) which are made from a novel 'Drop Stitch' inflatable panel material. On board the CABs are systems which can generate a variety of simulated signal influences to initiate the mine harmlessly away from ships. The system is controlled remotely at a safe distance on a nearby ship or even many miles away on land.

In December 2021, the MoD announced plans for the future acquisition of further elements of MHC programme that will see two of the three original units operating in United Kingdom waters, based at Portsmouth and Faslane, with the third deployed to the Gulf, probably from the dedicated in-theatre RFA Landing Ship Dock. The system is readily deployable from shore, Royal Navy, RFA or even commercial vessels. Each mission system consists of a Portable Operations Centre, an Autonomous Surface Vessel, towed sonar, mine neutralisation system, autonomous underwater vehicles, and an autonomous mine sweeping system.

Block II will comprise of a larger, as yet unspecified number of MHC Mission Systems that will make up the bulk of the replacement units to replace the Sandown Class by 2025. The investment decision point is currently planned for some time in 2024.

As the Royal Navy has decided to gradually move to autonomous minewarfare technology, we will see minewarfare experts from Sandown-class vessels being re-trained to operate the new autonomous minehunters and their associated state-of-the-art hunting and sweeping equipment. Controlled remotely these autonomous minehunters can be used to detect and classify mines or ordnance dumped in the sea at speed, without putting sailors and a multi-million-pound warship in danger.

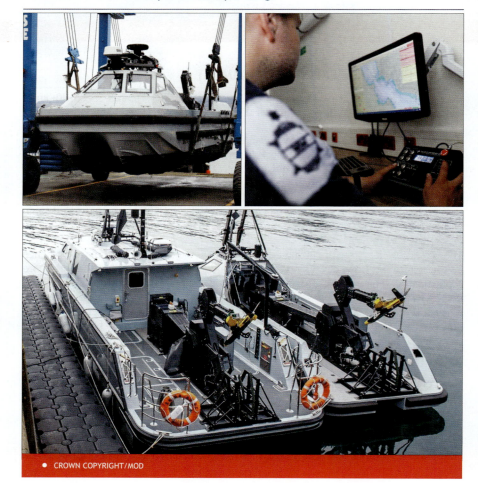

• CROWN COPYRIGHT/MOD

CROWN COPYRIGHT/MOD

REMUS 300 AUTONOMOUS UNDERWATER VEHICLES (SAUVs)

Displacement: N/A **Dimensions:** N/A **Payload:** N/A **Speed:** 5 knots **Complement:** None

Notes: Designed and developed by the American defence contractor Huntington Ingalls Industries (HII) the REMUS 300 autonomous underwater vehicle is being introduced into Royal Navy service to support mine-countermeasures operations. Initially they will be used on the remaining Hunt-class mine-countermeasure vessels to deliver what is known as a 'full spectrum' find-fix-finish capability at a range of depth profiles up to 300 metres.

REMUS 300 will also be used to help define the characteristics of the Royal Navy's next-generation Mine Hunting Capability (MHC) while also usefully being completely interchangeable with the same capability being developed by the US Navy.

Each REMUS 300 can be manoeuvred by a two man team and can be deployed for up to 20 hours with power being provided by a lithium-ion battery. The vehicles have a service speed of up to 5 knots.

CROWN COPYRIGHT/MOD   HMS Spey

PATROL VESSELS
RIVER II CLASS

Ship	Pennant Number	Completion Date	Builder
FORTH	P222	2018	BAE Systems
MEDWAY	P223	2019	BAE Systems
TRENT	P224	2019	BAE Systems
TAMAR	P233	2019	BAE Systems
SPEY	P234	2019	BAE Systems

Displacement: 2,000 tonnes **Dimensions:** 90.5m x 13.5m x 3.8m **Speed:** 24 knots **Armament:** 1 x 30mm cannon; 2 x Miniguns, 2 x GPMG **Aviation:** Flight deck capable of receiving aircraft up to Merlin size **Complement:** 36 (accommodation for 70)

Notes: The River II Class were developed from the previous River Class but are significantly more advanced and larger vessels with far greater capabilities including the addition of a flight deck capable of accommodating a Merlin helicopter; a capability that has been evaluated on MEDWAY during her current Caribbean deployment.

Each of the River IIs feature enhanced firefighting equipment, BAEs CMS-1 combat management system, an I Band Doppler SharpEye radar for helicopter control and improved accommodation. In fact, the bridge of a River II-class patrol vessel compares extremely favourably against a Type 45 destroyer or Type 23 frigate with plenty of space for personnel. Each of the five River II class ships have been painted in traditional dazzle colour schemes reminiscent of World War convoy escorts.

British Warships & Auxiliaries 2024

TAMAR and SPEY are deployed to the Pacific providing a constant RN presence in the region, although without any permanent shore facilities being made available for the two ships. They will instead victual at ports of opportunity and at naval bases of allies and friendly nations. MEDWAY continues to operate in the Caribbean providing a permanent presence in that region.

FORTH remains in service as the dedicated Falkland Islands Guardship and TRENT in the Mediterranean.

CROWN COPYRIGHT/MOD — HMS Trent

British Warships & Auxiliaries 2024

• DEREK FOX HMS Severn

PATROL VESSELS
RIVER CLASS

Ship	Pennant Number	Completion Date	Builder
TYNE	P281	2002	Vosper T
SEVERN	P282	2003	Vosper T
MERSEY	P283	2003	Vosper T

Displacement: 1,677 tonnes **Dimensions:** 79.5m x 13.6m x 3.8m **Machinery:** 2 MAN 12RK 270 diesels, 11,063 hp; 2 shafts; bow thruster **Speed:** 20+ knots **Armament:** 1 x 20mm; 2 x GPMG **Complement:** 48

Notes: These three ships were originally ordered from Vosper Thornycroft in 2001 on a then unusual deal whereby the Royal Navy leased them from the shipbuilder for five years at a cost of £60 million. A £52 million lease extension was agreed in January 2007 running to the end of 2013. The Ministry of Defence in 2012 authorised the purchase of the three ships from the shipbuilder for the price of £39 million.

The MoD intended to keep them operational for another ten years through to 2022. For a while it was expected that the new RIVER II-class would replace them in service and SEVERN was decommissioned in October 2017, but with the current Government's foreign policy statement on having dispersed naval assets around the globe, the RIVER IIs have been forward deployed leaving their older, smaller, and less capable, sister ships to maintain the round the clock protection of Great Britain's borders and vital Fishery Protection Role.

In November 2018, it was announced that the future of these three ships was secure for some time, but their future, or any replacements, other than the five RIVER IIs are unclear at the present time.

MERSEY, TYNE and SEVERN have a wide variety of taskings including escorting foreign warships passing through UK waters, conducting fishing vessel inspections and defending the UK border. Increasingly, they have also been used during the current illegal immigrant crisis in the English Channel.

The vessels also have an unique role in providing training for navigators from 700X Naval Air Squadron, who use the ships for testing their latest remotely-piloted Puma air system. With a range beyond 10 miles and an endurance of more than two hours, the Puma can vastly increase the ability of a ship to gather intelligence. Flying up to 45 miles per hour, the drones combine a high-tech control system with their array of sensors, including a times-fifty optical zoom, to live-stream video back to the ship. 700X Naval Air Squadron conducts its own training programme to prepare personnel for the Puma flights. The squadron also teaches military personnel from across defence in the use of quadcopters. It also researches and evaluates a wide range of remotely-piloted systems as the sector continues to increase.

• CROWN COPYRIGHT/MOD   **Puma Air System**

CROWN COPYRIGHT/MOD HMS Blazer

COASTAL TRAINING CRAFT
P2000 CLASS

Ship	Pennant Number	Completion Date	Builder
EXPRESS	P163	1988	Vosper T
EXPLORER	P164	1985	Watercraft
EXAMPLE	P165	1985	Watercraft
EXPLOIT	P167	1988	Vosper T
ARCHER	P264	1985	Watercraft
BITER	P270	1985	Watercraft
SMITER	P272	1986	Watercraft
PURSUER	P273	1988	Vosper T
TRACKER	P274	1998	Ailsa Troon
RAIDER	P275	1998	Ailsa Troon
BLAZER	P279	1988	Vosper T
DASHER	P280	1988	Vosper T

British Warships & Auxiliaries 2024

Ship	Pennant Number	Completion Date	Builder
PUNCHER	P291	1988	Vosper T
CHARGER	P292	1988	Vosper T
RANGER	P293	1988	Vosper T
TRUMPETER	P294	1988	Vosper T

Displacement: 54 tonnes **Dimensions:** 20.8m x 5.8m x 1.8m **Machinery:** 2 Caterpillar C18 diesels, 1,746 hp; 2 MTU diesels, 2,000 hp (TRACKER); 2 shafts **Speed:** 20 knots **Armament:** 3 x GPMG (Faslane-based vessels) **Complement:** 5 (with accommodation for up to 12).

Notes: These fourteen vessels are among the oldest Royal Navy units dating from the mid-1980s, but there are currently no plans for their replacement. Their role is to train future command personnel and most of the class are attached to University Royal Naval Units (URNU) but can also contribute to numerous other naval tasks around the waters of the United Kingdom and into European waters.

Vessels are assigned to the following URNUs, ARCHER (East Scotland); BITER (Manchester & Salford), BLAZER (Southampton); CHARGER (Liverpool); EXAMPLE (Northumbria); EXPLOIT (Birmingham); EXPLORER (Yorkshire); EXPRESS (Wales); PUNCHER (London); RANGER (Sussex); SMITER (Oxford); TRUMPETER (Cambridge).

RANGER and TRUMPETER were formerly allocated to the Gibraltar Squadron for guard ship and search and rescue duties, but were replaced by the dedicated Scimitar-class patrol boats. Unlike the remainder of the class, both these ships remain capable of being mounted with a 20mm cannon. In 2020, DASHER and PURSUER replaced the Scimitar-class SCIMITAR and SABRE as the Gibraltar Squadron.

SCIMITAR and SABRE were shipped back to the United Kingdom where they supplemented the training role performed by the ARCHER P2000 boats with University Royal Naval Units. They have been removed from service and were sold in September 2022. In 2021, DASHER and PURSUER were replaced by the new Gibraltar Fast Patrol Boats (see following page) constructed on Merseyside by Marine Specialist Technology.

DANIEL FERRO — HMS Cutlass

GIBRALTAR SQUADRON FAST PATROL BOATS

Ship	Pennant Number	Completion Date	Builder
CUTLASS	P295	2021	Marine Specialised Tech
DAGGER	P296	2022	Marine Specialised Tech

Displacemen:t 35 tonnes **Dimensions:** 19m in length **Machinery:** 3x Volvo D13-1000 engines driving 3x MJP350X waterjets **Speed:** up to 40 knots **Armament:** 3 x General Purpose Machine Guns (fitted for but not with 0.50cal Heavy Machine Gun) **Complement:** 6

Notes: These two vessels are the replacements for SCIMITAR and SABRE. In July 2020, the Ministry of Defence contracted Merseyside-based boat builder Marine Specialised Technology (MTS) to build a pair of new boats for the Gibraltar Squadron in a deal worth £9 million. Both boats are used to patrol HMNB Gibraltar and British Gibraltar Territorial Waters (BGTW) as well as supporting British exercises and operations in the area, keeping a close watch over Gibraltar's shores.

HMS CUTLASS arrived at Gibraltar on board the general cargo ship DEO VOLENTE on 15 November 2021. DAGGER joined her in April 2022, after a host of sea trials and safety checks, before being able to fly the White Ensign. The trials were completed in the middle of 2022.

The Gibraltar Squadron also operates a trio of Rigid Hull Inflatable Boats (RHIBs) and the recently allocated River II-class patrol ship TRENT.

• DANIEL FERRO HMS Scott

SURVEY SHIPS
SCOTT CLASS

Ship	Pennant Number	Completion Date	Builder
SCOTT	H131	1997	Appledore

Displacement: 13,500 tonnes **Dimensions:** 131.5m x 21.5m x 8.3m **Machinery:** 2 Krupp MaK 9M32 diesels, 10,800 hp; 1 shaft, CP propellor; retractable bow thruster **Speed:** 17 knots **Complement:** 78

Notes: It was feared that SCOTT would end her Royal Navy career in 2024/25 after having been granted a two year extension to her service life. Indeed, the ship had been listed for sale on the MoD's Defence Sales Authority's list of available equipment for foreign sales. In late May 2023 that listing was sensationally rescinded, and the decision taken to keep the ship in the fleet for another ten years out to 2033. The reasons behind this decision are manyfold. Firstly, the decommissioning of the two Echo-class survey ships to pay for the introduction of 'maturing' autonomous surveying equipment and the need to maintain a credible traditional ocean surveying capability led to the Ministry of Defence's retaining the SCOTT well past her expected 25 year service life. It does, however, mean that to keep the ship operational for longer, she will require an extensive mid-life LIFEX refit that will cost millions of pounds and will require the ship essentially to be gutted and rebuilt with new engines, new electronics and other equipment.

Built in 1997, SCOTT is the Royal Navy's last remaining dedicated ocean going survey ship. She was built to commercial standards and continues to provide extremely accurate and detailed deep bathymetric surveys of the continental shelf. She is fitted with modern multi-beam sonar suite with which she can conduct ocean mapping operations on a global scale. On board her 78 crewmembers operate a three-watch system whereby the ship is run by 48 of her crew with the remainder on leave at any given time. Each person aboard works 75 days on the ship before having 30 days ashore. In this way SCOTT can remain at sea for more than 300 days a year consolidating the work she has undertaken and avoiding unnecessary wasteful breaks in the surveying. She can navigate through thin Ice Class 1A conditions but only with the assistance of a dedicated icebreaker.

SCOTT is the largest survey vessel in Western Europe, and the fifth largest vessel in the Royal Navy. Named for the famous Arctic explorer Robert Falcon Scott, she also has an auxiliary role as a mine countermeasures vessel. In her 24 years at sea, the ship has surveyed approximately 3.7 per cent of the world's oceans alone – impressive when you consider that only one fifth of the world's oceans have been surveyed to modern standards.

Following a multi-million refit at Falmouth SCOTT sailed on a 15-month deployment in July 2022. Among the destinations visited during this last year were the United States and Gibraltar.

CROWN COPYRIGHT/MOD HMS Scott

HMS Protector

ICE PATROL SHIP PROTECTOR

Ship	Pennant Number	Completion Date	Builder
PROTECTOR	A173	2001	Havyard Leirvik (Norway)

Displacement: 4,985 tonnes **Dimensions:** 89.7m x 18m x 7.25m **Machinery:** 2 Rolls Royce Bergen diesels, 9,602 hp; 1 shaft; CP propellor; bow and stern thrusters **Speed:** 15 knots **Armament:** Miniguns; GPMGs **Complement:** 88 (accommodation for up to 100)

Notes: PROTECTOR is the Royal Navy's only Ice Patrol Ship and is usually found operating in the freezing waters of Antarctica and the Southern Hemisphere. PROTECTOR's ship's company includes a team of permanent divers who undertake exploratory surveys. The vessel spent five-months in dry dock in Teeside in 2020 being extensively overhauled and upgraded including the creation of a new quarterdeck structure with a naval stores complex, new workshops to maintain the ship's two small survey craft JAMES CAIRD IV and the 8.5m Rigid Work Boat TERRA NOVA. Interestingly, due to its previous civilian career, PROTECTOR is one of only two RN/RFA vessels fitted with a sauna. As Britain's dedicated Ice Patrol Ship PROTECTOR is usually found in the Southern Oceans, but the impact of global warming on the planet is having an arguably greater impact in the Arctic and in 2022 the ship visited northern polar regions for the second time in two years to conduct scientific experiments and to chart the loss of the ice cap as the planet warms. As part of this mission the ship has worked with drone experts from 700X Squadron from Culdrose to equip PROTECTOR with 'eyes in the sky' in the form of Evolve Dynamics' Sky Mantis drones. These aircraft can be used to identify areas of ice concentration and 'leads' – gaps in the ice through which she can safely navigate. The drones can also assist with aerial scientific survey work.

CROWN COPYRIGHT/MOD — HMS Magpie

INSHORE SURVEY VESSEL

Ship	Pennant Number	Completion Date	Builder
MAGPIE	H130	2018	Safehaven

Displacement: 37 tonnes **Dimensions:** 18m x 6.2m x 1.4m **Machinery:** 2x Volvo D16 diesels, 524 hp; 2 shafts **Speed:** 23 knots **Complement:** 12

Notes: MAGPIE replaced GLEANER in 2018 and has since then been actively surveying the inshore waters around the United Kingdom. She was purchased as one of 38 new workboats supplied by Atlas Elektronik and is unique in having a catamaran hull. She can operate offshore for up to 7 days with a crew of 12 and has a range of 1,400 nautical miles.

One of MAGPIE's first major taskings after commissioning in June 2018 was a continuation of work done by her predecessor GLEANER in surveying Portsmouth Harbour to ensure the stability of the seabed in anticipation of Portsmouth's use by the aircraft carriers QUEEN ELIZABETH and PRINCE OF WALES.

In March 2020 she was extensively updated with new software and electronics to keep her at the forefront of surveying technology. In 2022 the diminutive MAGPIE conducted a three-month survey of the River Tyne before sailing north to Scotland for a series of extensive surveys. She will also play a key role in the development of future capability by testing remote and autonomous systems along with other techniques to better collect and exploit environmental data.

• DEREK FOX   Patrick Blackett

NAVYX SUPPORT VESSEL

Ship	Pennant Number	Completion Date	Builder
PATRICK BLACKETT	X01	2022	Damen Group

Displacement: 270 tonnes **Dimensions:** 41.2m x 8.7m x 3m **Machinery:** 4 x Caterpillar C32 Ascert diesel engines **Speed:** 23 knots **Armament:** None **Complement:** 5

Notes: This unique £9 million adapted Fast Crew Supplier 4008 (FCS 4008), designed and built by Damen Group, was acquired by the Royal Navy to test and evaluate state-of-the-art modern technologies, particularly autonomous systems as they are developed for maritime use. The steel hulled/aluminium superstructure vessel is based on the Damen SCF 4008 design but adapted for British use and was purchased under the NavyX programme.

She has been equipped to operate the Royal Navy's PODS (Persistently Operationally Deployed System) which is located on the large cargo deck of the ship. She will also be infinitely adaptable for specific trials and experiments be they underwater, surface or aerial in nature. Some tests will be less visible to the casual observer as it is expected that she will also evaluate Artificial Intelligence warfighting solutions. She is named after the British physicist and Noble Prize winner Patrick Blackett, who made a major contribution in World War Two advising on military strategy and developing operational research.

PATRICK BLACKETT is painted matt black, rather than the Royal Navy's standard Pusser's Grey, complete with NavyX insignia on both sides of the hull. Her pennant, X01, is also uniquely highlighted in gloss paint and large QR codes are painted to either side of her superstructure, allowing smartphone users to scan them and view NavyX content.

• CROWN COPYRIGHT/MOD   Madfox

NAVYX MADFOX
UNMANNED SURFACE VESSEL

MADFOX standing for Maritime Demonstrator For Operational eXperimentation, was accepted into the Royal Navy in 2021 after being evaluated by the Defence Science and Technology Laboratory (Dstl) over a period of eighteen months. Based on the L3Harris Mast-13 autonomous vessel, MADFOX will be further evaluated by the Royal Navy in a variety of real-life scenarios to examine how autonomous vessels can deliver force multipliers, force protection and surveillance and reconnaissance assets to the fleet. For this next phase in its assessment process the vessel will be under the control of the NavyX organisation that is tasked with evaluating new and innovative pieces of equipment for the Royal Navy.

NAVYX is also currently evaluating an autonomous Rigid Inflatable Boat (RIB) that will be incorporated into the inventory of the future Type 26 and Type 31 frigates.

• CROWN COPYRIGHT/MOD   Madfox

British Warships & Auxiliaries 2024

CROWN COPYRIGHT/MOD   DBS Vulcan

DIVE SUPPORT BOATS

Ship	Pennant Number	Completion Date	Builder
DSB Vulcan	--	2023	Atlas Elektronik
DSB Volcano	--	2023	Atlas Elektronik
DSB Orcadian	--	2023	Atlas Elektronik
DSB Crabb	--	2023	Atlas Elektronik
TBC	--	2023	Atlas Elektronik
TBC	--	2023	Atlas Elektronik

Displacement: 25.51 tonnes **Dimensions:** 15m x 4.4m x 0.794m **Machinery:** Twin engine water jet propulsion **Speed:** 25 knots **Armament:** None **Complement:** 4

Notes: Six boats have been procured to improve the support given to Royal Navy divers. Replacing outdated vessels, the 15m Vahana boats provide improved speed, operational range and navigation equipment – all vital to diving operations. The £51 million project has seen the boats delivered over five years and the sixth and final one has now been handed over. Two of the vessels are based at the Defence Dive School in Portsmouth, with the others operated by the Fleet Diving Units in Portsmouth, Plymouth and Scotland. One of the boats is also working in Gibraltar.

Defence Equipment and Support (DE&S), the procurement arm for the Ministry of Defence, awarded a £51 million contract to Dorset-company Atlas Elektronik in 2017 to deliver the Vahana workboat programme over a five-year period, which includes these six vessels. These vessels are used by the military but are not officially listed as military assets.

• CROWN COPYRIGHT/MOD HMS Victory

HMS VICTORY

Ship	Completion Date	Builder
VICTORY	1758	Chatham Dockyard

Displacement: 3,500 long tonnes **Dimensions:** 57m x 15.8m x 8.76m **Armament:** 104 breach loaded cannon (non-operational)

Notes: HMS VICTORY remains a commissioned warship of the Royal Navy. She was built at Chatham Dockyard as a first-rate ship of the line. Originally commissioned in 1758. As of 2024, she boasts an impressive service record spanning 246 years, solidifying her status as the world's oldest operational naval vessel, although she will never again put to sea.

She is celebrated for her pivotal role as Lord Horatio Nelson's flagship during the renowned Battle of Trafalgar on 21st October 1805. Throughout her extensive career, she also served as the flagship for notable figures such as Keppel at the Battle of Ushant, Howe at Cape Spartel, and Jervis at the Battle of Cape St Vincent. In 1824, she was relegated to being a harbour training ship.

In 1922, the decision was made to relocate her to a dry dock in Portsmouth where she has remained meticulously preserved as a museum ship. Since 2012, she has also held the position of serving as the flagship of the First Sea Lord. VICTORY is in the process of being fully restored in a multi-million restoration programme that has uncovered the extent of how time and the maritime environment has affected her timbers. As one of the world's oldest surviving warships the millions of pounds being poured into her restoration will ensure her continued survival.

Royal Marine Craft

CROWN COPYRIGHT/MOD

The first records of Royal Marines were founded by King Charles II on 28 October 1664, but it wasn't until 1802 that they were given the name Royal Marines by King George III. In those 359 years the RM has earned a reputation for supreme bravery and excellence which continues to this day.

2021 saw a radical transformation of the force's structure, role and uniforms as it transformed into The Future Commando Force (FCF). The process saw the injection of £40 million into the Royal Marines and British amphibious capabilities. The Future Commando Force is swift, agile, and nimble and able to deploy rapidly around the globe at short notice. They are equipped with unique 'game changing' technology, weaponry and equipment unlike that used in any other units in the British armed forces and be capable of undertaking roles ranging from humanitarian aid, combat missions to full-scale warfighting. They will regularly deploy on attachment to the UKs' Carrier Strike Groups but also be retained in home waters. In July 2020, the Royal Marines created The Vanguard Strike Company, a unit of more than 150 Marines and British Army Commandos. But, some things are unchanged, including the spiritual home of the Commandos at Plymouth even if the FCFs' focus will increasingly become one of technical specialist operations.

To achieve the aim of increased agility personnel will work in 'small, versatile teams' specially tailored for each individual mission. Each Marine will be specially selected by individual skill sets allowing more autonomy of movement and decision at the company level. This could be as small as teams of four as was tested by 40 Commando in 2020 at Bovington Training Area in Dorset.

The Government's focus on forward deploying British forces abroad also applies to the Future Commando Force, with the aim of establishing high readiness groups in warships and auxiliaries already on deployment.

The Royal Marines will continue to operate landing craft from the assault ships BULWARK and ALBION and the Bay-class landing ships. Furthermore, they have a range of small fast inshore boats and assault craft on which Royal Marine personnel are trained at Plymouth, Instow in North Devon and at HMS Raleigh at Torpoint. The latter location houses the Royal Navy School of Board and Search, which trains personnel in the special skills of boarding vessels underway that may restrict searches.

The Royal Navy has 15 Reserve Units and a Fleet Diving Squadron consisting of 10 Units. The Royal Marines consists of 3 Commando Brigade, the Royal Marine Band Service, the Commando Training Centre and 4 Reserve Units.

• CROWN COPYRIGHT/MOD

ISLAND CLASS PATROL VESSELS

Ship	Pennant Number	Launch Date	Builder
RONA	-	2009	Holyhead Marine
MULL	-	2010	Holyhead Marine
EORSA	-	2014	Holyhead Marine

Displacement: 19.9 tonnes **Dimensions:** 14.9m x 4.6m x 0.9m **Machinery:** 2 Caterpillar diesels, 715 hp; 2 waterjets **Speed:** 33 knots **Armament:** 4 x GPMG **Complement:** 3

Notes: The Island-class patrol boats RONA and MULL were former Ministry of Defence Police vessels from the Clyde Marine Unit at HMNB Clyde, handed over to the Royal Marines in 2013. They were fitted with three new weapons mounts, extra protection and communications equipment and transferred to 43 Commando Fleet Protection Group Royal Marines for operation on the Clyde to escort high value units such as the Vanguard-class submarines. A third vessel, EORSA, was delivered direct from the builders. (An Island-class patrol vessel is pictured on the left in the photograph).

British Warships & Auxiliaries 2024

CROWN COPYRIGHT/MOD

Landing Craft Utility (LCU)

LCU Mk10

Ship	Pennant Number	Parent Unit	Builder
9730	1001	47 CRGRM	Ailsa, Troon
9731	1002	47 CRGRM	Ailsa, Troon
9732	1003	HMS ALBION	BAE Systems
9733	1004	HMS ALBION	BAE Systems
9734	1005	HMS ALBION	BAE Systems
9735	1006	HMS ALBION	BAE Systems
9736	1007	47 CRGRM	BAE Systems
9737	1008	47 CRGRM	BAE Systems
9738	1009	47 CRGRM	BAE Systems
9739	1010	47 CRGRM	BAE Systems

Displacement: 240 tonnes **Dimensions:** 29.82m x 7.7m x 1.70m **Machinery:** 2 MAN Diesels; 2 Schottel propulsors; 1 bow thruster **Speed:** 10 knots **Armament:** 2 x GPMG **Complement:** 7

Notes: LCU Mk10 (Landing Craft Utility) are operated by the Royal Marines and are a Ro-Ro style landing craft designed to operate from Albion-class LPDs or Landing Ship Dock Auxiliary (LSDA). Ordered in 1998 from Ailsa Troon, the fleet currently consists of ten vessels, with the first two delivered in 1999 and with the final vessels being accepted into service in 2003. The remainder were built by BAE Systems at Govan. Both ALBION and BULWARK are each capable of carrying four LCUs.

They have a 'drive-through' configuration, with ramps fore and aft and pilot house shifted to starboard. They are capable of transporting up to 120 fully equipped troops, one main battle tank or four large vehicles. With a range of around 600 nautical miles – more if auxiliary tanks are added – they are designed to operate independently for 14 days with a seven man Royal Marine crew in both arctic and tropical climates. All the crew members have bunk accommodation and there is a galley and store rooms.

CROWN COPYRIGHT/MOD — Mexeflote

Mexeflote
Dimensions: 38.66m x 12.4m x 1.54m **Speed:** 6.5 knots **Complement:** 6 Crew

Notes: The Mexeflote consists of multiple cells and engines that can be configured to provide a causeway, landing craft or Ramp Support Pontoon. It is capable of transferring vehicles and equipment up to 198 tonnes and is routinely deployed worldwide via LSDs of the Royal Fleet Auxiliary. The Mexeflote is the largest logistic landing craft in the military and is operated exclusively by the Royal Logistic Corps. The Mexeflote is highly versatile and has been deployed in support of the majority of operational deployments since the Falklands conflict.

CROWN COPYRIGHT/MOD

HMS Diamond

CROWN COPYRIGHT/MOD

Landing Craft Vehicle and Personnel (LCVP)

LCVP Mk5B

Ship	Pennant Number	Parent Unit	Builder
0202	B5	47 CRGRM	Babcock Marine
0203	NM	HMS ALBION	Babcock Marine
0204	B6	47 CRGRM	Babcock Marine
0205	P7	47 CRGRM	Babcock Marine
0338	T6	47 CRGRM	Babcock Marine
0339		HMS ALBION	Babcock Marine
0340	N2	HMS ALBION	Babcock Marine
0341	P9	47 CRGRM	Babcock Marine
0344		47 CRGRM	Babcock Marine
0345		47 CRGRM	Babcock Marine
0346	N3	HMS ALBION	Babcock Marine
0347		47 CRGRM	Babcock Marine
0353		47 CRGRM	Babcock Marine

Ship	Pennant Number	Parent Unit	Builder
0354		47 CRGRM	Babcock Marine
0355		47 CRGRM	Babcock Marine
0356	B8	47 CRGRM	Babcock Marine

Displacement: 24 tonnes **Dimensions:** 15.70m x 4.2m x 0.90m **Machinery:** 2 Volvo Penta diesels; 2 waterjets **Speed:** 25 knots **Armament:** 2 x GPMG **Complement:** 3

Notes: Designed to carry personnel and small vehicles, the first LCVP Mk5 (Landing Craft Vehicle and Personnel) was ordered in 1995 from Vosper Thornycroft and handed over in 1996. A further four were delivered in December 1996 with two more for training at RM Poole ordered in 1998. A further 16 were ordered from FBM Babcock Marine in 2001 with the final vessels being accepted into service in 2004. The Mk 5 can transport 8 tonnes of stores or a mix of 2 tonnes and 35 fully equipped troops, and operate from both ALBION and BULWARK. These vessels represent a significant improvement in capability over the preceding Mk4s with a greater range, lift and speed. They feature aluminium hulls and are powered by twin waterjets. Their design includes a rigid and enclosed windowed canopy and a ramp at the bow that lowers for rapid unloading. GPMGs can be mounted when needed. The primary role is the landing of vehicles, personnel and equipment onto potentially hostile shores. The secondary role is a general purpose support craft both between ships and ship to shore. The craft are capable of performing normal duties in conditions up to sea state 4 and run for cover up to sea state 5. Pennant numbers and parent units can change as the vessels are rotated through maintenance cycles. Under current plans these craft will be retired from service by 2027.

CROWN COPYRIGHT/MOD — Landing Craft Vehicle and Personnel (LCVP)

• CROWN COPYRIGHT/MOD

FUTURE COMMANDO INSERTION CRAFT

Notes: The Royal Marine Commandos have relied on legacy Mk 5B landing craft for a generation, but in the future they will have new purpose designed, stealthy Commando Insertion Craft (CIC) instead. The new craft will be built under the Commando Force modernisation programme. The new craft will be unlike the traditional landing craft currently in service and will be capable of carrying a strike team together with a small vehicle from 150 miles distant at 25 plus knots and crucially to have a low observable profile, meaning enemy radars will have problems locking on to the boats.

The RM's recapitalisation programme will see much of its inventory of vessels replaced over the coming decade with the United Kingdom's Defence and Security Accelerator (DASA) issuing a Novel Amphibious Craft competition out to industry for them to conceptualise new and innovative technologies and designs to meet an increasingly challenging maritime assault environment. It is expected that the competition will start towards the end of 2024 with a final decision on the construction of over 20 selected vessels to be awarded at the end of 2025. The expected cost would be somewhere in the region of £191 million.

Offshore Raiding Craftt

OFFSHORE RAIDING CRAFT (ORC)

Weight: 3.6 tonnes **Dimensions:** 9.1m x 2.9m x 0.66m **Machinery:** Twin Steyr MO256K43 250 bhp @ 4200rpm **Propulsion:** Rolls Royce FF270 Waterjets **Speed:** 36 knots **Armament:** 1x HMG/GPMG forward, 2 x GPMG/HMG/GMG/Minigun aft **Complement:** 2 and 8 troops

Notes: The Royal Marines operate two versions of the Offshore Raiding Craft (ORC), the Troop Carrying Variant (TCV) and Fire Support Variant (FSV). The ORC is an air portable surface manoeuvre craft designed for the rapid deployment of 8 fully equipped troops and 2 crew from over the horizon (30 miles) ship-to-shore and vice versa. They provide rapid movement of troops in coastal, estuarine, riverine and inland waters. The ORC has an aluminium hull with a low draught to allow for safe, rapid beach insertions. To provide ballistic protection for her 2 crew and passengers optional armour panels can be fitted. She can be transported as under-slung load by Chinook and Merlin helicopters or air-transported inside a C130 Hercules transport plane. Around 39 ORCs are in service with the Royal Marines. The ORC is manufactured by Holyhead Marine of Anglesey, North Wales.

RIGID RAIDING CRAFT

Notes: The Royal Marines operate a large number of smaller Rigid-hulled and Rigid-Inflatable Craft for various assault, patrol and security duties. There are 5.2, 6.5 and 8 metre long versions. Rigid Raiders feature GRP (glass reinforced plastic) hulls and early variants featured single or twin outboard motors. A small team of men can carry the boats, even with engines attached, due to their lightweight construction. They can also be air-dropped out to sea. The latest RRC, the Mk3, is powered by a 240 hp inboard diesel engine but the Royal Marines might start replacing these with ORCs. They can carry up to eight troops. Rigid Raiders are manufactured by RTK Marine (now part of BAE Systems).

• DEREK FOX   **Fast Insertion Craft**

SPECIALIST CRAFT

In addition to the familiar Rigid Raiding Craft and Rigid Inflatable Boats other specialist vessels are available including the Fast Interceptor Craft (FIC) with a top speed of 60 knots. Back in July 2007 it was revealed that the Special Boat Service (SBS) were to take delivery of the so-called 'stealth boat'. The vessel is manufactured by Portsmouth-based VT Halmatic, which is now part of BAE Systems, but not much has been revealed about the vessel. The vessel has been spotted numerous times in waters off Poole, home of the SBS, and according to the BAE Systems Maritime website they are currently in service with UK Special Forces.

To maintain a low radar cross-section, external fittings such as raydomes, aerial fits and apertures on the craft are kept to a minimum. This results in low radar and heat signatures enabling a stealth capability. The specification of the boats in service with the UK Special Forces remain a mystery as there are numerous options not only for the propulsion lines (such as twin or triple petrol outboards through to twin diesel stern drives, twin diesel jet drives or twin Arneson surface drives) but also for the system facilities. Options include multiple fuel tank arrangements, water separator/primary filter within the engine compartment, electric and manual bilge systems with automatic sensing and high bilge alarms, fire and/or smoke detection system with visual/audible display on console and/or cabin, variety of navigation and communication systems available to end user specification, including, but not limited to, fully integrated intercom systems, radar, satcom and multiple radio installation.

All craft are air transportable with special trailers available to suit different aircraft including A400M, C130 and C17.

Three models are available 30, 40 and 180.
Dimensions - Model 30: 10.75m x 2.59m x 0.7m
Dimensions - Model 40: 13.07m x 2.83m x 0.82m
Dimensions - Model 180: 18.1m x 3.8m x 0.9m

• US NAVY   Swimmer Delivery Vehicle

SWIMMER DELIVERY VEHICLES

Swimmer Delivery Vehicles (SDV) are miniature submarines operated by Britain's Special Forces to insert commandos and others into frontline situations or to undertake clandestine work. The Royal Navy owns three SDV Mk8 Mod 1 versions which are used by the Special Boat Service.

The Mk8 is the same vehicle used by the United States Navy SEAL teams, although the SEALs are upgrading their SDVs with the Shallow Water Combat Submersible (SWCS), designated as the Mk 11 SDV. In 2018 the UK government announced the intention to purchase three replacement SWCS for their existing fleet of SDVs.

On January 14, 2021, the US Department of Defense announced that a foreign military sale request from Teledyne Brown Engineering, the manufacturers of the SWCS, for around USD39 million firm-fixed price modification to an existing contract had been awarded. The buyer nation was not disclosed due to the secretive nature of the technology involved but is widely believed to be to honour the British contract.

Ships for the Future Fleet

BABCOCK INTERNATIONAL

ASTUTE CLASS SUCCESSOR - SSN(R) - AUKUS

The follow-on attack submarine to the Astute Class has been on the drawing board since 2018 with the foundation of the Maritime Underwater Future Capability (MUFC). This committee was tasked with formulating the Royal Navy's future course of travel set against a backdrop of world developments but pegged by realistic economies within the British defence budget. MUFC didn't have an auspicious start. As soon after the Initial Concept Phase was started the programme was suspended for two years to allow personnel to focus their attention on the Dreadnought and overrunning Astute programmes instead.

The next mention of MUFC came in the Integrated Defence Review with a name change to SSN(R). The construction programme was not expected to start anytime sooner than the late 2030s due to build limitations at BAE Systems Barrow shipyard and the existing workload at the shipyard. What was known at the time was that the new increasingly stealthy submarines would be up to 25 per cent larger than the already large Astute-class submarines and that unmanned systems would play an increasing part in its armament and sensor outfit. Power would be from a Rolls Royce PWR-3 nuclear reactor and a specialist hangar for a Chalfont-type Deep Dive System might be incorporated into the design. Another design feature often quoted is that the SSN (R)s would be fitted with an X-tail instead of the more traditional Royal Navy single tail and rudder. These larger boats will need the dry-docks at Devonport, where they will be refitted, extended, enlarged and modernised.

The tri-lateral pact between Australia, United States and the United Kingdom to develop a submarine to satisfy the needs of the Royal Australian Navy was announced in San Diego by US President Joe Biden, UK Prime Minister Rishi Sunak and Australian Prime Minister Anthony Albanese on 13 March 2023. The Australians wanted to replace their fleet of Collins-class conventionally powered submarines with something that could stand up to the challenge posed by a rapidly expanding Chinese Navy in Southeast Asia.

Initially they chose to build conventionally powered French-designed submarines and even inked a deal with NAVAL Group for the delivery of these boats. Australia would later, controversially, pull out of the deal and instead go with the nuclear option proposed by the United States and the United Kingdom.

Under the terms of the AUKUS agreement Australia will acquire three or four American Virginia-class attack submarines, probably from existing units of the US Navy, although it is unclear at present which submarines or when they may be transferred to the Royal Australian Navy. At the same time, personnel from Australia will be trained by both the USN and RN in the operation of nuclear submarines at sea during foreign exchanges and at nuclear ship operation schools ashore. As the Royal Australian Navy learns how to operate their 'second-hand' Virginia-class vessels, both the UK and Australia will have finalised the designs of the AUKUS successor submarines which will be built at BAE Systems shipyard at Barrow-in-Furness. The Royal Navy and Royal Australian Navy vessels will be built alongside one another on a production line.

The AUKUS deal is extremely controversial, particularly with China, who viewed the nuclearisation of Australia as provocative. In the United Kingdom while welcomed, the deal did raise questions about how BAE Systems would deliver the submarines as currently each Astute-class submarine takes an average six to seven years to build.

TYPE 83 DESTROYERS

The integrated Defence Review highlighted the need to lay long-term ambitions to replace the current fleet of Type 45 Air Defence Destroyers in the late 2030 – early 2040 timeframe. Current thinking is to develop a version of the Type 26 frigate to perform this role originally known as the T4X project. 2021's Defence Command Paper stated that the United Kingdom will build a new class of warships with the aim being that 'the concept and assessment phase for our new Type 83 destroyer which will be begin to replace our Type 45 destroyers in the late 2030s'.

The use of a variant of a pre-existing design could prove to be a wise idea as it will cut design and development time and could create a continuous stream of shipbuilding in the United Kingdom for the Royal Navy. If the Royal Navy were to replace the Daring Class with six Type 83s this could see the aim of continuous shipbuilding in Glasgow on the Type 26 production line extending beyond the eight Type 26s already ordered or projected. In February 2022, the MoD announced that the design effort behind the Type 83 destroyer would consider the threat posed by Hypersonic missile systems when designing these new expensive vessels. What these measures are remains uncertain.

TYPE 32 FRIGATES

First announced on 19 November 2020 as part of a defence investment pledge prior to the Integrated Review. Whereas the Type 26 frigates will make up the high end of the technological mainstream of the fleet, Type 32s would be designed primarily to act in defence of the territorial or littoral waters around Great Britain and provide 'persistent presence' in support of the new Littoral Response Groups (LRGs).

Much of the design work on the Type 32 has yet to be completed but what is known is that former Defence Minister Ben Wallace envisaged these ships to function as a 'platform for autonomous systems' and used in the widest variety of roles from anti-submarine warfare to mine countermeasures activities. They will also share a common heritage with the Type 26 and Type 31e in that they will be of modular design and general purpose in focus with the construction work expected to go to Scottish shipyards.

In 2023 there was speculation that the class might not be ordered at all and be delayed as a defence economy. This suggestion was flatly refuted by the Ministry of Defence who said that the class was still a priority and was at an advanced stage of design.

FLEET SOLID SUPPORT REPLACEMENT PROGRAMME

On 16 November 2022 Team Resolute, one of the bidders for the construction of three Fleet Solid Support Ships, comprising of BMT, Harland and Wolff and Navantia UK, were appointed as the preferred bidder to deliver these critically required new vessels to the Royal Fleet Auxiliary. The contract worth £1.6 billion will, if exercised, provide a trio of modern supply ships and crucially the majority of the work will be completed within the United Kingdom supporting British shipbuilding.

Spanish-owned Navantia UK will be the prime contractor who will transfer cutting edge digital shipyard knowledge to Harland and Wolff in Belfast. This technology transfer element of Team Resolute's proposal is said to have been one of the deciding factors in awarding the contract to the team. Some components will be manufactured in Spain, but the vast majority will be fabricated in the United Kingdom and final assembly and commissioning will be at Harland and Wolff. Construction of the new ships, based on the British BMT design, will begin as soon as the £77 million investment into Harland and Wolff's shipyard facilities is completed. The pressing need, however, remains that RFA FORT VICTORIA still needs to be replaced by 2028. The other two new ships are expected to enter service by 2032.

NATIONAL FLAGSHIP

In November 2022, it was announced that plans to build a new National Flagship, what many refer to as a new 'Royal Yacht', were scrapped. The vessel was going to be named after the late Prince Philip. Former Secretary of State for Defence Ben Wallace told MPs that he would instead prioritise the procurement of the Multi-Role Ocean Surveillance Ships (MROSS) instead of the flagship.

The proposed National Flagship, which would assume much the same role and purpose as the former Royal Yacht BRITANNIA, decommissioned in 1997, would be built in the UK with the stated aim of reinvigorating British shipbuilding.

It would have been the first vessel of its kind in the world, reflecting the UK's burgeoning status as a great, independent maritime trading nation. Every aspect of the ship, from its build to the businesses it showcases on board, would have represented and promoted the best of British – a clear and powerful symbol of commitment to be an active player on the world stage. As well as promoting trade, it was expected that the flagship would play an important role in achieving the UK's foreign policy and security objectives, including by hosting summits and other diplomatic talks.

• CROWN COPYRIGHT/MOD

FUTURE SOLID SUPPORT SHIPS

Displacement: 39,000 tonnes **Dimensions:** 216m x 34.5m **Range:** 11,000 nautical miles **Machinery:** TBC **Speed:** 19 knots **Complement:** 101

Notes: In November 2022 the Team Resolute consortium was awarded the contract to construct three Solid Support ShipS to reinvigorate the moribund state of the Solid Support ships in the Royal Fleet Auxiliary. After years and years of indecision and kicking the decision into the long grass the award came as welcome relief to the service which had seen the two 1970s built Fort-class ships sold to Egypt and the 1990s built FORT VICTORIA soldiering on despite her advancing years and increasing maintenance costs.

In design the new ships will be similar in profile to the Tide-class tanker and will feature 3 replenishment rigs, which is fewer than many had expected plus a RASCO sited amidships and container handling capabilities forward. There will be space on board each of the three ships for 9,000 square metres of cargo space. Interestingly, as a cost saving measure the port side RAS stations will not both align with the rigs fitted on QUEEN ELIZABETH and PRINCE OF WALES.

As part of their winning bid to build these three vessels, Team Resolute will invest £77 million into the British shipbuilding industry at Harland and Wolff in Belfast and at Appledore in North Devon. Another £21 million in technology transfer skills will be provided from the Spanish shipbuilder Navantia. Navantia's participation in the programme was slightly controversial as large sections of the new ships will be constructed in Spain and brought to Belfast for final assembly.

The first FSS will, when work starts sometime in 2025, be the first naval vessel built in Belfast since 1993 when RFA FORT VICTORIA was completed. All three FSS will, it is hoped, be operational by 2032.

• BMT TECHNOLOGY

MULTI-ROLE SUPPORT SHIPS (MRSS)

The Ministry of Defence has a stated aim to acquire a small force of Multi-Role Support Ships (MRSS) with the operational role being 'to provide the platforms to deliver Littoral Strike, including Maritime Special Operations, in the early 2030s'. In the past the MoD had wanted to produce two specialist ships - the Littoral Strike Ship (LSS) alongside the new Fleet Solid Support Ships (FSSS) but the former class now appears to have been abandoned. The UK's amphibious and littoral capability at present rests with two Albion-class assault ships and four Bay-class Landing Platform Docks. Both classes are due to be withdrawn by the early 2030s and will need to be replaced. The Royal Navy is following US Navy doctrine closely as it develops both a carrier strike and a littoral strike capability in parallel.

The MRSS programme is intended to provide the Royal Navy and Royal Marines with the ability to transport and deliver troops, vehicles, equipment and supplies anywhere in the world and then support them once in theatre. Such vessels will have a range of specialist capabilities including a large flight deck, replenishment-at-sea capabilities and landing craft.

There is a danger in trying to design the ships to try and achieve too much in one design. Time and again, designers who attempt too much in a single leap forward create white elephants that fail to achieve the desired aims. In general terms the MRSS will be a large, 200 metre long, vessel with large reserves of space for the accommodation of troops, a floodable well deck and a flight deck capable of accommodating the largest military helicopter in British service, the RAF's Boeing Chinook's heavy-lift helicopters.

In July 2023 the UK and Dutch governments came together to try and design and develop new assault ships for the two navies.

Royal Fleet Auxiliary

CROWN COPYRIGHT/MOD

RFA Argus

Auxiliary vessels are as important and in some cases, more important than the warships they serve. In each auxiliary ship governments and navies have invested time, money and resources into building a system that keeps navies at sea for prolonged periods and to extend the range and reach of a country's military and economic might. Around the globe in the last five years there has been an almost feverish construction boom in naval auxiliaries. The Royal Fleet Auxiliary has not been exempted - with the delivery of the four excellent Tide-class tankers, but as other countries commit to constructing newer, better, faster and larger more capable tonnage, the Ministry of Defence dithers over how best to provide the service with the new ships it needs to deliver dry stores to the fleet.

The MARS programme has been stymied by the usual governmental ineptitude and lack of decision making, while the existing ships are driven on for longer past their shelf life. MARS should have delivered the three planned solid stores ships by now, but in 2021, when a new round of bids were expected to have been sought, nothing has been announced. To be fair the government has been waging a war of sorts against the COVID-19 pandemic and its focus has not been on delivering future capability to the Armed Forces, but a decision must be made soon, after all it takes at least three years to build new ships in the United Kingdom, the Government's stated aim. Less if the Government breaks another promise and has them built overseas against the findings of their own National Shipbuilding Programme.

Today the Royal Fleet Auxiliary is, like the Royal Navy it serves, a shadow of its former scale, complexity and capability. Yet, the ships in this 'fleet within a fleet' often substitute for warships which are needed elsewhere in the world. It is common for a tanker or supply ship to be positioned in the Caribbean during hurricane season or off the West Coast of Africa as a safeguard against the unavailability of the precise and limited number of warships in the Royal Navy.

That being said, the Royal Fleet Auxiliary Service in 2023 (118 years since its formation in 1905), is the backbone that keeps the Royal Navy at sea and supplied with everything from fuel, ammunition, food and 'nutty' (sweets and snacks).

CROWN COPYRIGHT/MOD — RFA Fort Victoria

SHIPS OF THE ROYAL FLEET AUXILIARY
Pennant Numbers

Ships	P. No.	Page
Tankers		
TIDESPRING	A136	87
TIDERACE	A137	87
TIDESURGE	A138	87
TIDEFORCE	A139	87
WAVE KNIGHT	A389	86
WAVE RULER	A390	86
Stores Ship/Tankers		
FORT VICTORIA	A387	88
Ocean Surveillance Vessel		
PROTEUS	K60	91

Ships	P. No.	Page
Amphibious Ships		
LYME BAY	L3007	89
MOUNTS BAY	L3008	89
CARDIGAN BAY	L3009	89
Primary Casualty Receiving Ship/Aviation Training Ship		
ARGUS	A135	90
Autonomous Mine Warfare Support Vessel		
STIRLING CASTLE	M01	92

● DEREK FOX RFA Mounts Bay

British Warships & Auxiliaries 2024

CROWN COPYRIGHT/MOD   RFA Wave Knight

FAST FLEET TANKERS
WAVE CLASS

Ship	Pennant Number	Completion Date	Builder
WAVE KNIGHT	A389	2002	BAE Systems
WAVE RULER	A390	2002	BAE Systems

Displacement: 31,500 tonnes (FL) **Dimensions:** 196.5m x 28.25m x 10m **Machinery:** Diesel-electric: 4 Wärtsilä DG, 25,514 hp (18.76 MW); 2 GEC Alstom motors with variable speed converters, 19,040 hp (14 MW); 1 shaft; 1 bow and stern thruster **Speed:** 18 knots **Armament:** 2 x Vulcan Phalanx, 2 x 30mm **Aircraft:** Up to 2 Merlin **Complement:** 80 (plus 22 Fleet Air Arm)

Notes: These two ships have a displacement of 31,500 tonnes and are powered by diesel electric propulsion. Each has three replenishment rigs on port and starboard and a Hudson reel type system at the stern. Capacity is 16,900 tonnes of fuel and 915 tonnes of dry stores. The large flight deck and associated hangar can accommodate a pair of Merlin sized helicopters which can be used for vertical replenishment. Both ships have a modern well-equipped medical facility, and their reverse osmosis system can provide 100m3 of fresh water every day. This facility has proven to be of immense value during humanitarian missions such as the annual hurricane season in the Caribbean where fresh water is one of the first essentials for survival.

RFA Tidesurge

FLEET TANKERS
TIDE CLASS

Ship	Pennant Number	Completion Date	Builder
TIDESPRING	A136	2017	Daewoo Shipbuilding
TIDERACE	A137	2018	Daewoo Shipbuilding
TIDESURGE	A138	2018	Daewoo Shipbuilding
TIDEFORCE	A139	2019	Daewoo Shipbuilding

Displacement: 39,000 tonnes (FL) **Dimensions:** 200.9m x 28.6m x 10m **Machinery:** 2 Wärtsilä diesels, 20,394 hp; 2 shafts **Speed:** 26.8 knots **Armament:** 2 x Phalanx CIWS; 2 x 30mm **Aircraft:** 1 x Merlin or Wildcat **Complement:** 63 (plus 26 spare berths)

Notes: At 39,000 tonnes displacement these four ships are the newest and largest ships operated by the Royal Fleet Auxiliary Service. Based on the AEGIR-26 design by BMT Defence Services, they are double-hulled to prevent oil escaping from any possible breaches in compliance with SOLAS (Safety of Life at Sea) regulations for the transportation of oil products around the globe. The ships were designed in parallel with the Queen Elizabeth-class aircraft carriers and their rigs and cranes are compliant with those of the aircraft carriers. Each ship has three abeam RAS(L) stations, one to port and two to starboard for diesel oil, aviation fuel and fresh water. A typical RAS transfer between ships weighs around two tonnes. During a replenishment-at-sea these ships can transfer up to 800 cubic tonnes of fuel an hour. The ships have a large flight deck and hangar for the operation of a single AugustaWestland Wildcat or Merlin helicopter for vertical replenishment operations.

CROWN COPYRIGHT/MOD

RFA Fort Victoria

REPLENISHMENT SHIPS
FORT CLASS II

Ship	Pennant Number	Completion Date	Builder
FORT VICTORIA	A387	1992	Harland & Wolff

Displacement: 33,675 tonnes **Dimensions:** 204m x 30m x 9m **Machinery:** 2 Crossley-Pielstick V-16 diesels, 23,904 hp; 2 shafts **Speed:** 20 knots **Armament:** 2 x 30mm Oerlikon / BMARC KAA guns in GAM-B01 mounts, 2 x Phalanx CIWS, 15 cell Sea Wolf Missile System (fitted for but not with) **Complement:** 95 RFA, 24 MoD Civilians, 15 RN and up to 154 Fleet Air Arm

Notes: FORT VICTORIA is a fleet tanker capable of worldwide operation in support of Royal Navy warships. Nominally available to the fleet, the ship has, however, been laid up since late 2021 with mechanical and crewing issues to blame. The 1993 built vessel is now entering into her fourth decade of service and is simply worn out. The biggest issue, however, is that she is, until the delivery of the new Fleet Solid Stores ships the only ship capable of resupplying the two RN aircraft carriers at sea. The RFA has been put into an awkward position over whether to refit the ship to provide this essential role until the new FSSs arrive or to scrap the ship. This in turn would lead to blunting the effectiveness of the aircraft carriers as they would not be able to independently deploy overseas without the support of a dedicated supply ship. Despite this, the MoD has stated that she will deploy with the Carrier Strike Group in 2025 to the Asia-Pacific region and that she will be refitted in 2024 to satisfy that role. She will eventually be replaced around 2028. Confirmation of the intention to acquire the new capability came in July 2022 when Rear-Admiral Paul Marshall, the Senior Responsible Officer for the Fleet Solid Support ship project, told the House of Commons Select Defence Committee that the lead ship of this class was envisaged for service entry in 2028.

RFA Cardigan Bay

LANDING SHIP DOCK (AUXILIARY) BAY CLASS

Ship	Pennant Number	Completion Date	Builder
LYME BAY	L3007	2007	Swan Hunter
MOUNTS BAY	L3008	2006	BAE Systems
CARDIGAN BAY	L3009	2007	BAE Systems

Displacement: 16,190 tonnes **Dimensions:** 176.6m x 26.4m x 5.8m **Machinery:** Diesel-electric; 2 Wärtsilä 8L26 DG, 6,000 hp (4.5 MW); 2 × Wärtsilä 12V26 DG, 9,000 hp (6.7 MW); 2 azimuthing thrusters; 1 bow thruster **Speed:** 18 knots **Armament:** 2 x Phalanx CIWS (exact weapons fit varies within the class) **Complement:** 60

Notes: These three amphibious landing ships can offload embarked troops and armoured vehicles from ship-to-shore using their assigned Landing Craft Vehicle Personnel (LCVP) and Landing Craft Utility (LCU) vessels. These ships are highly versatile and can operate in extremely rough conditions to support amphibious operations and ground forces around the globe.

In 2020 the MoD's intention was to convert one of the Bay-class ships into a Littoral Strike Ship (LSS). Two years later it appears that this plan may have been abandoned as the focus of the LSS conversation has shifted to repurposing the Aviation Training Ship RFA ARGUS to fulfil this emerging role.

Currently out of service dates are MOUNTS BAY (2031), CARDIGAN BAY (2031) and LYME BAY (2032).

CROWN COPYRIGHT/MOD RFA Argus

PRIMARY CASUALTY RECEIVING SHIP/ AVIATION TRAINING SHIP

Ship	Pennant Number	Completion Date	Builder
ARGUS	A135	1981	Cantieri Navali Breda

Displacement: 28,481 tonnes (Full Load) **Dimensions:** 175.1m x 30.4m x 8.1m
Machinery: 2 Lindholmen Pielstick 18 PC2.5V diesels, 23,400 hp; 2 shafts; 1 bow thruster
Speed: 18 knots **Armament:** 4 x 30mm, 2 x 20mm **Aircraft:** up to 6 Merlin
Complement: 254 (inc 137 FAA)

Notes: ARGUS is the United Kingdom's Primary Casualty Receiving/Aviation Training Ship in which capacity she operates an extensive Role 3 100 bed medical facility complete with CT scanner and radiology research and dentistry operating theatre. The care facility operates with a staff of up to 250 doctors, nurses and support staff. As the ship is armed (2 x Oerlikon 20mm/85 KAA on GAM-B01 mountings and 4 x 7.62mm GPMGs Mk44 Miniguns) and is not painted in the required white and red crosses, the Geneva Convention prevents her from being officially classified as a hospital ship. Her aviation training role is crucial in allowing new naval helicopter pilots at-sea experience of landing on the pitching and rolling deck at sea in comparative safety. However, the construction of a casualty evacuation lift, together with a deckhouse aft of the superstructure, has reduced helicopter capability by one landing spot. Before the Russian invasion of Ukraine, it was intended that the 42 year-old ARGUS would be retired from service in 2024 without replacement. In July 2022 it was announced that the ship would be retained for another six years until 2030. In July 2022, it was reported that ARGUS could assume the future UK Littoral Strike Role after a refit to convert her to this role. In late 2023 ARGUS was deployed to the Mediterranean as part of Britain's response to the Hamas Terrorist groups attacks against innocent Israelis. Her presence, and that of LYME BAY, was as a contingency as her hospital facilities and helicopters could have proved useful in any escalation.

- SERCO　　　　　　　　　　　　　　　　　　　　　　　　　　　　　　　RFA Proteus

OCEAN SURVEILLANCE VESSEL

Ship	Pennant Number	Completion Date	Builder
PROTEUS	K60	2019	Vard

Displacement: 6,133 tonnes (Full Load) **Dimensions:** 98.1m x 20.05m x 6m **Machinery:** Azimuth Propulsion pods **Speed:** TBC **Armament:** Fitted for but not necessarily with light weapons **Complement:** 98 (mix of RFA and RN personnel)

Notes: The former offshore ocean vessel MV TOPAZ TANGAROA was purchased in early 2023 from Topaz Marine for £70 million. She arrived at Cammell Laird shipyard in late January for conversion to meet Ministry of Defence standards which will require the ship to be painted grey and fitted with mounts for military armaments (for but not necessarily with) and military standard communications equipment.

RFA PROTEUS commissioned into service whilst alongside the World War Two cruiser HMS BELFAST in London. The ship is fitted with a large deck space aft, a heavy lift craft, a helipad and crucially a moonpool in the centre of the ship for the launch and retrieval of underwater reconnaissance and surveillance equipment. PROTEUS is extremely manoeuvrable with her azimuth propulsion and Global Positioning System allowing her to maintain her position with great accuracy.

• DEREK FOX

RFA Stirling Castle

AUTONOMOUS MINE WARFARE SUPPORT VESSEL

Ship	Pennant Number	Completion Date	Builder
STIRLING CASTLE	M01	2013	Vard

Displacement: 5,840 tonnes (Full Load) **Dimensions:** 96.8m x 20m x 4.6m **Machinery:** Liquid Natural Gas Propulsion **Speed:** 13.6 knots **Armament:** Fitted for but not necessarily with light weapons **Complement:** up to 100 personnel can be accommodated

Notes: MV ISLAND CROWN was purchased as a direct result of increasing concern over the threat posed to the UK's extensive subsea infrastructure, such as telecommunications, energy powerlines and pipelines, and the 2022 Russian invasion of Ukraine.

In February 2023 she was bought to be converted, initially at HMNB Devonport into a mothership for new and innovative mine countermeasure operations with autonomous mine vessels. Her early service with the Royal Fleet Auxiliary has been dominated by trials deploying Mine Countermeasure Maritime Autonomous Systems (MCM MAS) and drones.

She became operational in May 2023 and in July 2023 conducted first trials with three of the Navy's autonomous vessels: Royal Navy motorboats APOLLO, HYDRA and HAZARD.

The vessel has a workable 561 square metre working deck, a helipad and accommodation spaces for up to 100 personnel. Due to her previous career as a civilian vessel STIRLING CASTLE is equipped with a sauna.

• NAVYBOOKS　　　　　　　　　　　　　　　　　　　　　　　MT Raleigh Fisher

COMMERCIAL TANKER

Ship	Completion Date	Builder
RALEIGH FISHER	2005	Guangzhou Shipyard, China
CUMBRIAN FISHER	2004	Samho Shipbuilding, Mason, S Korea

Displacement: 22,184 tonnes (GRT); 35,191 tonnes (DWT) **Dimensions:** 172m x 28m x 8.3m **Machinery:** 2SA 5 cylinder Burmeister & Wain diesel, 9,721 hp; 1 shaft; bow thruster **Speed:** 14.5 knots

Notes: In 2019 Maersk took their remaining vessels off the UK Ship Register, exiting the UK Tonnage Tax and ending the training of UK cadets, and sold the tanker MAERSK RALEIGH to UK-based James Fisher & Sons for £9 million. Nick Henry, James Fisher chief executive, said that the renamed tanker - RALEIGH FISHER - would be significant for their tanker business as the vessel is presently contracted to the Ministry of Defence to support the Royal Navy's fuelling needs, both in the UK and abroad, on a five-year contract. The MoD charters the vessel to commercial companies when it is not in use for their own requirements. RALEIGH FISHER is the ex ROSA MAERSK and was renamed and reflagged (to UK flag) in August 2017.

CUMBRIAN FISHER is currently sailing under a Bahamian flag and is occasionally used by the MoD to transfer chemical products. She has a displacement of 8,446 tonnes, with a speed of 10 knots and is much smaller with a length of 127.2m x 20.43m x 6.1m.

Both vessels will be used to move fuel products between the UK, the Falkland Islands and Cyprus, where the MoD supplies RAF Akrotiri with jet fuel. RAF Akrotiri is located on the southern tip of Cyprus and is the service's busiest base.

● GORDON BRODIE   MV Hartland Point

STRATEGIC SEALIFT RO-RO VESSELS
POINT CLASS

Ship	Pennant Number	Completion Date	Builder
HURST POINT		2002	Flensburger
HARTLAND POINT		2002	Harland & Wolff
EDDYSTONE		2002	Flensburger
ANVIL POINT		2003	Harland & Wolff

Displacement: 10,000 tonnes, 13,300 tonnes (FL) **Dimensions:** 193m x 26m x 7.6m
Machinery: 2 MaK 94M43 diesels, 21,700 hp; 2 shafts; 2 CP propellors; 1 bow thruster
Speed: 18 knots **Complement:** 18-22

Notes: In late 2021 the UK Ministry of Defence began to investigate possible future strategic sealift options with the aim of introducing new shipping in 2025. The first stage of the process was to invite interested commercial shipping companies to bid to offer an interim capability for a minimum of five years. The current 25 year private finance initiative (PPI) sealift contract with Foreland Shipping runs until December 2024.

The Request for Proposals sets out what the MoD expects in terms of ship characteristics, classification, capacities, and crew requirements. It also requests information on any previous long-term charter/contract arrangements and the ability to provide 'surge' capacity at short notice when required. Full operational capability under the new contract is planned for January 2025.

CROWN COPYRIGHT/MOD

Serco Marine Services

- SERCO

SD Powerful

Around the coastal waters of the United Kingdom and at several overseas establishments you are likely to see smaller support craft that provide vital facilities to make for the safe and efficient operation of the Royal Navy. These vessels are operated by Serco. Serco have been supporting the Royal Navy since 1996 and provide an end-to-end vessel provisioning service which includes vessel design and acquisition, technical management and operations of a varied fleet of new builds, legacy vessels, conversions and chartered vessels.

Amongst the specialist tasks undertaken by Serco operated vessels are: training support by providing vessels suitable for Royal Navy training, helicopter search and rescue training and the development and deployment of a range of ROVs via the mothership capability delivered by SD NORTHEN RIVER. One of the principal roles of the SERCO operated fleet is towage in and outside the three naval bases at Devonport, Portsmouth and Faslane plus the transportation of personnel and VIPs from shore bases to warships at sea. In 1996 SERCO inherited a collection of legacy specialist vessels that are increasingly coming to the end of their service lives and the company has an active programme to find innovative solutions to acquire new build or legacy vessels to replace them.

On 16 November 2022 Serco was awarded a contract by the UK Ministry of Defence (MoD) to continue to provide marine services for the Royal Navy. Following the end of the 15-year private finance initiative (PFI) arrangements for the provision of marine services, the ownership of the vessels reverted back to the MoD, and the new agreement was with the Royal Navy directly. The contract, which is valued at around £200 million, will last for 27 months commencing in December 2022 and follows on directly from the current PFI, ensuring continuity of support. The MoD has an option to extend the contract for up to six months.

SHIPS OF SERCO MARINE SERVICES

Ship	Page	Ship	Page
SD ADEPT	102	SD PADSTOW	110
SD ANGELINE	114	DSM POPPY	115
SD BOUNTIFUL	101	SD POWERFUL	102
SD BOVISAND	109	SD RAASAY	114
SD CAREFUL	102	SD RELIABLE	101
SD CATHERINE	106	SD RESOURCEFUL	101
SD CAWSAND	109	SD SOLENT RACER	116
SD CHRISTINA	104	SD SOLENT SPIRIT	116
SD CLYDE RACER	116	SD SUZANNE	104
SD DEBORAH	104	SD TAMAR RACER	116
SD DEPENDABLE	101	SD TAMAR SPIRIT	116
SD EILEEN	104	SD TEESDALE	112
SD ENGINEER	114	SD TEMPEST	99
SD FAITHFUL	102	SD TILLY	106
SD FLORENCE	105	SD VICTORIA	107
SD FORCEFUL	102	SD WARDEN	108
SD GENEVIEVE	105	SD WATERPRESS	112
SD HERCULES	103		
SD IMPETUS	98		
SD IMPULSE	98	**Briggs Sub-Contract**	
SD INDEPENDENT	100		
SD INDULGENT	100	CAMERON	117
SD INSPECTOR	114	KINGDOM OF FIFE	117
SD KYLE OF LOCHALSH	108		
SD MARS	103	SMIT DEE	118
SD MOORFOWL	115	SMIT DART	118
SD MOORHEN	115	SMIT DON	118
SD NAVIGATOR	114	SMIT YARE	118
SD NETLEY	110	SMIT SPEY	118
SD NEWHAVEN	110	SMIT STOUR	119
SD NORTHERN RIVER	113	SMIT ROTHER	119
SD NORTON	111	SMIT ROMNEY	119
SD NUTBOURNE	110	SMIT CERNE	119
SD OBAN	111	SMIT FROME	119
SD OCEANSPRAY	112	SMIT MERRION	119
SD OILMAN	112	SMIT PENALLY	119
SD OMAGH	111	SMIT WEY	119
SD ORONSAY	111	SMIT NEYLAND	119

Entries displayed in lighter typeface have been removed from contract and are awaiting sale.

JOHN CRAE SD Impulse

TUGS

IMPULSE CLASS

Ship	Completion Date	Builder
SD IMPULSE	1993	Richard Dunston (Hull)
SD IMPETUS	1993	Richard Dunston (Hull)

G.R.T.: 319 tonnes **Dimensions:** 32.5m x 10.5m x 5.2m **Machinery:** 2 Allen 8S12 F-BC diesel engines; 3,400 hp; 2 Azimuth thrusters; 1 bow thruster **Speed:** 12 knots **Complement:** 5

Notes: Designed and built specifically to service the Vanguard-class ballistic missile submarines at Faslane with both vessels entering service in 1993, these tugs are used to manoeuvre submarines within the Clyde area and can provide additional services during trials and exercises. IMPULSE was in February 2018 completely modernised for further service. Serco has delayed the decision on both vessel's future and will make this in 2024 or soon thereafter.

● DEREK FOX   SD Tempest

ART 8032 CLASS

Ship	Completion Date	Builder
SD TEMPEST	2017	Damen (Poland)

G.R.T.: 495 tonnes **Dimensions:** 32.9m x 13.2m x 6.2m **Machinery:** 3 Caterpillar 3512C diesels, 5,295 kW; 3 Schottel SRP 1215 CP propellors **Speed:** 13 knots **Complement:** 4

Notes: With a bollard pull of 82 tonnes TEMPEST is the most modern and most powerful tug in the Serco fleet. She was acquired to serve the two Queen Elizabeth-class aircraft carriers at Portsmouth, but when not used in that capacity she provides general harbour towage services. She was ordered in February 2016 and launched in Gdansk (Poland) on 14 September 2016. In February 2017 she arrived at Portsmouth - her homeport.

To facilitate her work with the carriers with their large overhangs TEMPEST is fitted with a foldable mast and is also fitted with a double drum render/recovery aft winch.

● DEREK FOX   SD Indulgent

ASD 2509 CLASS

Ship	Completion Date	Builder
SD INDEPENDENT	2009	Damen (Netherlands)
SD INDULGENT	2009	Damen (Netherlands)

G.R.T.: 345 tonnes approx **Dimensions:** 25.14m x 9.44m x 4.45m **Machinery:** 2 Caterpillar diesels; 3,500 hp; 2 RR thrusters; 1 bow thruster **Speed:** 13 knots **Complement:** 4

Notes: Both these vessels are homeported at Portsmouth and provide general harbour towage services to warships based there. Each tug has a bollard pull of 40 tonnes and powered by a pair of Azimuth thrusters mounted at the stern. They are frequently seen at Portsmouth cold moving ships around the various stations, a role for which they have been especially fitted out.

• DEREK FOX SD Bountiful

ATD 2909 CLASS

Ship	Completion Date	Builder
SD RELIABLE	2009	Damen (Netherlands)
SD BOUNTIFUL	2010	Damen (Netherlands)
SD RESOURCEFUL	2010	Damen (Netherlands)
SD DEPENDABLE	2010	Damen (Netherlands)

G.R.T.: 271 tonnes **Dimensions:** 29.14m x 9.98m x 4.41m **Machinery:** 2 Caterpillar diesels; 4,025 hp; 2 RR thrusters **Speed:** 13.1 knots **Complement:** 4 (Portsmouth); 5 (Clyde)

Notes: Built in Poland by the Dutch firm Damen these four Azimuthing Tractor Drive (ATD) tugs are some of the most manoeuvrable tugs in the Serco fleet. Based on a standard Dutch design the four vessels were especially modified for British service with the addition of two double drum towing winches, extensive underwater fendering, fire fighting equipment and space and facilities to carry passengers and a limited number of stores. SD BOUNTIFUL is based at Portsmouth. SD RESOURCEFUL, SD RELIABLE and SD DEPENDABLE are all based on the Clyde.

• SERCO   SD Faithful

TWIN UNIT TRACTOR TUGS

Ship	Completion Date	Builder
SD ADEPT	1980	Richard Dunston
SD CAREFUL	1982	Richard Dunston
SD FAITHFUL	1985	Richard Dunston
SD FORCEFUL	1985	Richard Dunston
SD POWERFUL	1985	Richard Dunston

G.R.T.: 384 tonnes **Dimensions:** 38.8m x 9.42m x 4m **Machinery:** 2 Ruston diesels; 2,575 hp; 2 Voith-Schneider propellors **Speed:** 12 knots **Complement:** 5

Notes: These vessels are the survivors of a larger class of naval harbour tugs that have become ubiquitous at Devonport, Portsmouth and on the Clyde since the mid-1980s. Despite their age these venerable tugs are still extremely capable, and some are likely to be refitted to prolong their service lives. SD Forceful is currently based at Clyde whilst all others are based at Devonport.

- SERCO SD Hercules

STAN TUG 2608 CLASS

Ship	Completion Date	Builder
SD HERCULES	2009	Damen (Netherlands)
SD MARS	2009	Damen (Netherlands)

G.R.T.: 133.92 tonnes **Dimensions:** 26.61m x 8.44m x 4.05m **Machinery:** 2 Caterpillar 3508B TA diesels; 2,200 hp; 2 Van de Giessen Optima nozzles; 90kW HRP hydraulically powered bow thruster **Speed:** 12 knots **Complement:** 4 (6 max)

Notes: The Stan Tug has, since their entry into service in 2009, proved to be a versatile conventional twin-screw tug ideal for coastal and port operations. For naval service, the tug has a comprehensive outfit of equipment enabling them to perform a wide variety of tasks in addition to standard towing operations. Each tug is fitted with two towing winches, a combined anchor windlass and single drum winch located on the foredeck and a double drum towing winch on the after deck. The class features a large and mostly empty deck space aft which has proven to be useful for handling submarine mounted towed array sonars. SD HERCULES is based at Devonport. SD MARS is currently being used on the Kyle of Lochalsh performing a variety of functions include towing and passenger transportation. In 2023 the MoD disposed of SD Jupiter.

• DEREK FOX SD Suzanne

ASD 2009 CLASS

Ship	Completion Date	Builder
SD CHRISTINA	2010	Damen (Poland)
SD DEBORAH	2010	Damen (Poland)
SD EILEEN	2010	Damen (Poland)
SD SUZANNE	2010	Damen (Poland)

G.R.T.: 120.74 tonnes **Dimensions:** 21.2m x 9.4m x 3.9m **Machinery:** 2 Caterpillar 3508B TA/C diesels; 2,000 hp; 2 Rolls Royce US 155CP thrusters **Speed:** 11 knots **Complement:** 5

Notes: Derived from the hugely successful Damen ASD (Azimuth Stern Drive) 2411 ship handling tug these four vessels have a bollard pull of 30 tonnes. Winches fore and aft, together with a bow thruster, make these tugs suitable for handling smaller surface ships, barge work and assisting with submarine movements, especially in the case of SD DEBORAH and SD EILEEN as the pair are based at Devonport. SD CHRISTINA and SD SUZANNE are based at Portsmouth.

JOHN DURSTON · SD Florence

FELICITY CLASS

Ship	Completion Date	Builder
SD FLORENCE	1980	Richard Dunston
SD GENEVIEVE	1980	Richard Dunston

G.R.T.: 88.96 tonnes **Dimensions:** 22.0m x 6.4m x 2.6m **Machinery:** 1 Mirrlees-Blackstone diesel; 615 hp; 1 Voith-Schneider CP propellor **Speed:** 10 knots **Complement:** 4 (Florence - 3)

Notes: Some of the oldest vessels currently in the Serco fleet, these three vessels were delivered between 1974 and 1980 and are used for the movement of small barges around harbours and ports. They have a bollard pull of 5.7 tonnes. SD GENEVIEVE is based at Portsmouth with SD FLORENCE currently located at Devonport. SD HELEN was disposed of by MoD a couple of years ago. Therefore it is likely that these will be amongst the first vessels replaced by new construction harbour craft.

PUSHY CAT 1204

Ship	Completion Date	Builder
SD CATHERINE	2008	Damen (Netherlands)

G.R.T.: 29.4 tonnes **Dimensions:** 12.3m x 4.13m x 1.55m **Machinery:** 1 Caterpillar 3056 TA diesel; 165 hp; 1 shaft **Speed:** 8 knots **Complement:** 2

Notes: SD CATHERINE is often seen operating within Portsmouth Harbour and is used as a general line runner and harbour workboat. She is powered by a single Caterpillar 3056 TA diesel driving a single screw. Additionally, she is fitted with a propulsion nozzle and twin rudders giving her a 2.1 tonnes bollard pull.

SD Tilly ● Mark Corner

STAN TUG 1405

Ship	Completion Date	Builder
SD TILLY	2009	Damen (Netherlands)

G.R.T.: 45 tonnes **Dimensions:** 14.55m x 4.98m x 1.8m **Machinery:** 2 Caterpillar diesels; 600 hp; 2 Van de Giessen nozzles **Speed:** 9 knots **Complement:** 3

Notes: Based at Devonport, SD TILLY is a general purpose inshore and harbour tug and is mostly used as a general workboat and line handler. Her design is an upgraded twin screwed version of the Pushy Cat 1204 with a larger and more powerful bow thruster giving her an 8 tonnes bollard pull capability.

• GEORGE EMMETT   SD Victoria

WORLDWIDE SUPPORT VESSEL

Ship	Completion Date	Builder
SD VICTORIA	2010	Damen (Romania)

G.R.T.: 3,522 tonnes **Dimensions:** 83m x 16m x 4.5m **Machinery:** 2 Caterpillar 3516B diesels; 4,000 hp; 2 shafts; CP propellors; 1 bow thruster **Speed:** 14 knots **Complement:** 16 (accommodation for 72)

Notes: SD VICTORIA was built in Romania at Damen's Galatz shipyard and at 83 metres in length is the second largest vessel in the Serco Marine Services fleet. She has twin controllable pitch propellors driven by a pair of Caterpillar 3516B diesel engines. She is based at Greenock's Great Harbour and was designed to provide a full range of services to support training missions anywhere around the globe. Although Serco Marine Services have her available for commercial charter she is mostly used in support of British military training and exercises. Inside the ship are large well-equipped spaces, set up as classrooms, briefing rooms and an operations room. Elsewhere onboard spaces have been allocated to workshop facilities. Her most notable feature is the large crane on the stern. There is provision to carry and operate a variety of small craft such as Rigid Inflatable Boats (RIBs), and forward of the bridge there is a helicopter winching deck.

TRIALS VESSEL

Ship	Completion Date	Builder
SD WARDEN	1989	Richards

Displacement: 626 tonnes **Dimensions:** 49m x 11m x 4m **Machinery:** 2 Ruston diesels; 4,000 hp; 2 shafts; CP propellors **Speed:** 15 knots **Complement:** 11

Notes: Serco Marine Services, as part of their contract with the Ministry of Defence, provide ships and facilities for trials of future equipment for the Royal Navy. In support of these activities Serco operates SD WARDEN out of the Kyle of Lochalsh. Her principal role, however, is to act as a Mooring and Weapons Recovery vessel at the British Underwater Test and Evaluation Centre (BUTEC) where her work supports the testing of future underwater weapon systems, sonar technologies and the evaluation of ships' radiated noise profiles in the water. In recent years SD WARDEN has been a focal point for the work undertaken by QinetiQ in the development of Remotely Operated Vehicles (ROVs). Serco has delayed decommissioning plans for SD WARDEN until 2024 or soon thereafter.

SD Warden • Michael Lennon

TRIALS VESSEL

Ship	Completion Date	Builder
SD KYLE OF LOCHALSH	1997	Abels Boatbuilders

Displacement: 120 tonnes **Dimensions:** 24.35m x 9m x 3.45m **Machinery:** 2 Caterpillar diesels; 2,992 hp; 2 shafts **Speed:** 10.5 knots **Complement:** 4

Notes: Built in 1997 by Abels Boatbuilders in Bristol as the twin-screw tug MCS LENIE, SD KYLE OF LOCHALSH has spent most of her career in the service of Serco Marine Services in Scottish waters. In 2008, after some years on contract, she was purchased from Maritime Craft Services (Clyde) Ltd and renamed. She has since been used in trials and operations at Kyle of Lochalsh. She has a bollard pull 26 tonnes.

● GORDON BRODIE   SD Cawsand

TENDERS
STORM CLASS

Ship	Completion Date	Builder
SD BOVISAND	1997	FBM (Cowes)
SD CAWSAND	1997	FBM (Cowes)

G.R.T.: 225 tonnes **Dimensions:** 23m x 11m x 2m **Machinery:** 2 Caterpillar diesels; 1,224 hp; 2 shafts **Speed:** 15 knots **Complement:** 5

Notes: These tenders have a distinctive appearance and are amongst the most frequently seen vessels darting around Plymouth harbour and up the River Tamar. They were bought at a cost of £6.5 million apiece and have a SWATH hull form (Small Waterplane Area Twin Hull) which offered improved performance. They are used to support the work of Flag Officer Sea Training (FOST) and with their relatively high speed can transfer staff quickly and comfortably to and from warships and auxiliaries within and beyond the confines of Plymouth breakwater.

NEWHAVEN CLASS

Ship	Completion Date	Builder
SD NEWHAVEN	2000	Aluminium SB
SD NUTBOURNE	2000	Aluminium SB
SD NETLEY	2001	Aluminium SB

Displacement: 77 tonnes (45 grt) **Dimensions:** 18.3m x 6.8m x 1.88m **Machinery:** 2 Cummins diesels; 710 hp; 2 shafts **Speed:** 10 knots **Complement:** 2/3 Crew (60 passengers)

Notes: The Newhaven Class uses a standard twin hull form and are generally utilised in the general passenger duties role within harbours and ports. SD NETLEY and SD NUTBOURNE are based at Portsmouth, while SD NEWHAVEN is currently located at Devonport where she operates in support of Flag Officer Sea Training (FOST). SD NEWHAVEN differs slightly from her two sisters as she has been modified (same modifications as SD Padstow) with strengthened forward bollard and with the addition of transfer wings to enable underway personnel transfers. Technically the Newhaven Class and Padstow Class are the same class.

SD Netley ● Derek Fox

PADSTOW CLASS

Ship	Completion Date	Builder
SD PADSTOW	2000	Aluminium SB

Displacement: 77 tonnes (45 grt) **Dimensions:** 18.3m x 6.8m x 1.88m **Machinery:** 2 Cummins diesels; 710 hp; 2 shafts **Speed:** 10 knots **Complement:** 2/3 Crew (60 passengers)

Notes: SD PADSTOW is another MCA IV, VI and VIA Passenger Vessel based at Devonport. Built in Hampshire by Aluminium Shipbuilders she has been modified along similar lines to SD NEWHAVEN in order to facilitate the speedy and safe transfer of personnel to other vessels whilst underway. Technically the Padstow Class and Newhaven Class are the same class.

OBAN CLASS

Ship	Completion Date	Builder
SD OBAN	2000	McTay Marine
SD ORONSAY	2000	McTay Marine
SD OMAGH	2000	McTay Marine

G.R.T.: 199 tonnes **Dimensions:** 27.7m x 7.30m x 3.75m **Machinery:** 2 Cummins diesels; 1,050 hp; 2 Kort-nozzles **Speed:** 10 knots **Complement:** 4 Crew (60 passengers)

Notes: Built to replace elderly tenders used since the 1970s, in 2000 this trio of vessels are MCA Class IIA Passenger Vessels. SD OBAN is primarily assigned the duties associated with Flag Officer Sea Training (FOST) and as such operates principally out of Devonport. SD ORANSAY and SD OMAGH are currently based on the Clyde and used mostly for general passenger duties but have a secondary role in the Cargo Ship VIII(A) role.

SD Norton • Mark Adams

PERSONNEL FERRY

Ship	Completion Date	Builder
SD NORTON	1989	FBM Marine

G.R.T.: 21 tonnes **Dimensions:** 15.8m x 5.5m x 1.5m **Machinery:** 2 Mermaid Turbo diesels; 280 hp; 2 shafts **Speed:** 13 knots **Complement:** 2

Notes: Conceived as the first of a projected series of vessels to replace the once numerous fleet tenders SD NORTON was a prototype vessel designed to carry 30 passengers or 2 tonnes of stores and has a relatively simple catamaran hull form. The projected extra vessels never materialised.

• DEREK FOX   SD Ocean Spray

COASTAL OILER

Ship	Completion Date	Builder
SD TEESDALE	1976	Yorkshire Drydock Co.

G.R.T.: 499 tonnes **Dimensions:** 43.86m x 9.5m x 3.92m **Speed:** 8 knots **Complement:** 5

Notes: SD TEESDALE is an oil products tanker that was taken up from commercial use by the company of John H Whitaker. In commercial service the ship was known as TEESDALE H. In Serco Marine service she is listed as a parcel tanker capable of delivering diesel and aviation fuel products together with delivering/receiving compensating water. She is self-propelled by two Aquamaster thrusters.

A Diesel Lighter Barge, SD OILMAN, and a Water Lighter Barge, SD WATERPRESS, are operated on the Clyde. A further barge, SD OCEANSPRAY, a Liquid Mixed Lighter Barge, is based at Portsmouth.

SD OILMAN has a displacement of 222 tonnes and is a Damen DBa 3009 lighter. She was built in Poland and completed by Damen in the Netherlands in 2009. She has a length of 30.4m, with a width of 8.5m and serves as a non-propelled barge. SD OCEANSPRAY is a 764 tonnes non-propelled barge with a length of 43.22m and a width of 15.4m. She was constructed by Crist in Gdansk, Poland and completed in 2010.

• SERCO SD Northern River

MULTI-PURPOSE VESSEL

Ship	Completion Date	Builder
SD NORTHERN RIVER	1998	Myklebust (Norway)

G.R.T.: 3,605 tonnes **Dimensions:** 92.8m x 18.8m x 4.9m **Machinery:** 2 Bergen diesels; 9,598 hp; 2 shafts; CP propellors; 2 bow thrusters **Speed:** 14 knots **Complement:** 14

Notes: SD NORTHERN RIVER is the largest vessel operated by Serco Marine Services and is listed as a multi-purpose auxiliary ship. In March 2012 she was bought from Deep Ocean AS and entered service with Serco to perform a wide range of support taskings including towing, boarding training and submarine escort. Built as an offshore support vessel she boasts a large open and flat work deck which can be quickly and easily modified to suit the tasks required through the installation of modulated palleted containers including specialist sonar equipment. NORTHERN RIVER can also conduct nuclear emergency and submarine rescue support missions. The latter requires the embarkation, fitting and operation of specialist ROVs, escape vessels and Transfer Under Pressure (TUP) facilities on the after deck, together with the embarkation of an additional 40 personnel.

MULTICAT 2510 CLASS

Ship	Completion Date	Builder
SD NAVIGATOR	2009	Damen (Netherlands)
SD RAASAY	2010	Damen (Netherlands)

Displacement: 362 tonnes **Dimensions:** 25.54m x 10.64m x 2.34m **Machinery:** 2 Caterpillar diesels; 957 hp; 2 shafts **Speed:** 8.4 knots **Complement:** 3 (plus up to 12 additional personnel)

Notes: SD NAVIGATOR is equipped for buoy handling with a single 9 tonnes capacity crane. She is capable of supporting diving operations. SD NAVIGATOR is managed from Devonport but operates between Devonport and Portsmouth. SD RAASAY is based at the Kyle of Lochalsh and is fitted with two cranes for torpedo recovery and support diving training. Two similar, but smaller vessels, SD INSPECTOR (ex-DMS EAGLE until March 2003 and ex-FORTH INSPECTOR until December 2007) and SD ENGINEER, operate from Portsmouth and Devonport respectively. SD INSPECTOR is a Utility Vessel that was built in 2001 with a length overall of 18.7m and a width of 8m. SD ENGINEER is a Work Vessel that was built in 1996 with a length overall of 17.49m and a width of 8.06m.

SD Navigator (Derek Fox)

MULTICAT 2613 CLASS

Ship	Completion Date	Builder
SD ANGELINE	2015	Damen (Netherlands)

Displacement: 657 tonnes **Dimensions:** 25.5m x 13.6m x 4m **Machinery:** 2 Caterpillar C32 TTA diesels; 2 Promarin fixed pitch propellors; bow thruster **Speed:** 10.1 knots **Complement:** Accommodation for 8 persons, consisting of four double crew cabins

Notes: SD ANGELINE was ordered in April 2014 and was accepted by the MoD in April 2015. Built at the request of the MoD to provide support in Faslane Naval Base primarily to submarines, but can undertake other naval base work. Her total power output is 2,850 kW with a bollard pull of 30.8 tonnes. The installed crane has a capacity of 15 tonnes.

DIVING SUPPORT VESSELS
MOOR CLASS

Ship	Completion Date	Builder
SD MOORFOWL	1989	McTay Marine
SD MOORHEN	1989	McTay Marine

Displacement: 518 tonnes **Dimensions:** 36m x 12m x 2m **Machinery:** 2 Cummins diesels; 796 hp; 2 Aquamasters; 1 bow thruster **Speed:** 8 knots **Complement:** 10

Notes: Designed as a powered mooring lighter for use within sheltered coastal waters, the lifting horns have been removed from the bows of both vessels when they were converted to Diving Support Vessels. They are used by the Defence Diving School for diving training in the Kyle of Lochalsh. Serco advises that the decommissioning plans for the Moor Class will be delayed.

SD Moorfowl • John Ashfields

CLYDE PILOT BOAT

Ship	Completion Date	Builder
DSM POPPY	2022	Holyhead Marine

Displacement: 24 tonnes **Dimensions:** 16.5m x 5.3m x 1.3mm **Machinery:** Twin Scania D176 - 650 BHP @ 1800 rpm **Speed:** 28 knots **Complement:** Accommodation for 5 to 10 persons

Notes: DMS POPPY is a Lloyds Register Class pilot boat built of glass reinforced plastic that will be used in the waters in and around the Clyde estuary and the approaches to HMS Neptune, the naval facility at Faslane by the King's Harbour Master.

STAN TENDER 1505 CLASS

Ship	Completion Date	Builder
SD CLYDE RACER	2008	Damen (Netherlands)
SD SOLENT RACER	2008	Damen (Netherlands)
SD TAMAR RACER	2008	Damen (Netherlands)

G.R.T.: 25.19 tonnes **Dimensions:** 15.2m x 4.8m x 1.25m **Machinery:** 2 Caterpillar diesels; 1,100 hp; 2 shafts **Speed:** 26 knots **Complement:** 2 (+ 8 Passengers)

Notes: Frequently seen operating within Royal Navy dockyards and approaches, these fast twin-screw workboats are built from strong aluminium. They regularly transfer pilots, VIPs and passengers to and from warships and can also undertake port security operations. Each boat's name gives an indication to which port they are assigned.

Derek Fox SD Solent Spirit

STAN TENDER 1905 CLASS

Ship	Completion Date	Builder
SD SOLENT SPIRIT	2008	Damen (Netherlands)
SD TAMAR SPIRIT	2008	Damen (Netherlands)

G.R.T.: 43.3 tonnes **Dimensions:** 19.2m x 5.3m x 1.8m **Machinery:** 2 Caterpillar diesels; 2,200 hp; 2 shafts **Speed:** 25 knots **Complement:** 2 (+ 10 passengers)

Notes: Steel hull with aluminium superstructure. Special propellor tunnels are fitted to increase propulsion efficiency and to reduce vibration and noise levels. These vessels are able to operate safely and keep good performance in wind speeds up to Force 6 and wave heights of 2 metres. Employed on transfer on pilots, VIPs and personnel. Each boat's name gives an indication to which port they are assigned. SD CLYDE SPIRIT was disposed of in 2023 by the MoD and replaced by DSM POPPY (see previous page).

- GORDON BRODIE
Kingdom of Fife

ANCHOR HANDLING TUG

Ship	Completion Date	Builder
KINGDOM OF FIFE	2008	Damen (Romania)

Displacement: 1,459 tonnes **Dimensions:** 61.2m x 13.5m x 4.75m **Machinery:** 2 Caterpillar diesels, 2,720 hp each; 1 shaft; bow thruster **Speed:** 13.7 knots **Complement:** 18

Notes: KINGDOM OF FIFE is operated by Briggs Marine under a 15-year £100 million contract from Serco to support navigation buoy maintenance and mooring support for the Royal Navy. This requires the company to regularly inspect, service and repair where necessary, over 350 moorings, navigation buoys and targets around the UK's coastline and those in the Falkland Islands, Gibraltar and Cyprus. A second vessel operated by Briggs Marine is the former Serco vessel CAMERON which can, when required, be fitted with a decompression chamber for teams of deep sea divers servicing the buoys and navigational aids.

- LEE HARRISON
Cameron

British Warships & Auxiliaries 2024

- GORDON BRODIE   Smit Dart

AIRCREW TRAINING VESSELS

Ship	Comp Date	Builder	Base Port
SMIT DEE	2003	BES Rosyth	Buckie
SMIT DART	2003	BES Rosyth	Plymouth
SMIT DON	2003	BES Rosyth	Blyth
SMIT YARE	2003	FBMA Cebu	Great Yarmouth
SMIT SPEY	2003	FBMA Cebu	Plymouth

G.R.T.: 95.86 GRT **Dimensions:** 27.6m x 6.6m x 1.5m **Machinery:** 2 Cummins diesels; 1,400 hp; 2 shafts; 1 centreline waterjet; 305hp **Speed:** 20 knots **Complement:** 6

Notes: The service for Marine Support to Range Safety and Aircrew Training is provided by SMIT International (Scotland) Ltd. A new seven year contract for £39m started in April 2018 and will run for five years until March 2023, with an option to extend for a further two years. These vessels provide support to aircrew training such as sea survival drills, various helicopter exercises, target towing and other general marine support tasks. They also participate in Navy Command sea training serials, particularly boarding exercises and force protection exercises involving fast attack craft scenarios. SMIT DART completed as a passenger vessel with a larger superstructure.

• IAN BOYLE Smit Neyland

RANGE SAFETY VESSELS

Ship	Comp Date	Builder
SMIT STOUR	2003	Maritime Partners Norway
SMIT ROTHER	2003	Maritime Partners Norway
SMIT ROMNEY	2003	Maritime Partners Norway
SMIT CERNE	2003	Maritime Partners Norway
SMIT FROME	2003	Maritime Partners Norway
SMIT MERRION	2003	Maritime Partners Norway
SMIT PENALLY	2003	Maritime Partners Norway
SMIT WEY	2003	Maritime Partners Norway
SMIT NEYLAND	2003	Maritime Partners Norway

G.R.T.: 7.0 GRT **Dimensions:** 12.3m x 2.83m x 0.89m **Machinery:** 2 Volvo Penta diesels; 680 hp; 2 Hamilton waterjets **Speed:** 28 knots **Complement:** 2

Notes: A class of 12m Fast Patrol Craft which provide a range safety service to 7 land based ranges across the UK. They also participate in Navy Command Sea Training serials including participation in Fast Attack Craft scenarios. Part of a £39 million contract the MoD awarded to SMIT International (Scotland) Ltd in April 2018.

• DEREK FOX   AWB Mistral

ARMY VESSELS
WORK BOATS

Vessel	Pennant Number	Completion Date	Builder
STORM	WB41	2008	Warbreck Eng.
DIABLO	WB42	2008	Warbreck Eng.
MISTRAL	WB43	2008	Warbreck Eng.
SIROCCO	WB44	2008	Warbreck Eng.

Displacement: 48 tonnes **Dimensions:** 14.75m x 4.30m **Machinery:** 2 John Deere Diesels; 402 hp; 2 shafts **Speed:** 10 knots **Complement:** 4

Notes: These work boats are part of the Army's strategic port operations in Southampton, but can be transported by a 'mother ship' to other ports and places like Iraq. Are often used as tugs for Mexeflotes, positioning other pontoon equipment and for handling flexible pipelines. They have a firefighting capability. The Army also operate a number of smaller Combat Support Boats. Built by RTK Marine/VT Halmatic (now BAE) these are fast and rugged small craft, 8.8m long with a twin Hamilton waterjet propulsion system powered by twin 210 hp diesel engines.

J M BRISCOE — Combat Support Boat

ARMY VESSELS
COMBAT SUPPORT BOAT

Displacement: 48 tonnes **Dimensions:** 8.77m x 2.90m x 0.60m **Machinery:** Combination of water jets and diesel inboard engines **Speed:** 27 knots

Notes: The Combat Support Boat is a powerful, versatile craft whose major role is to support both bridging and amphibious operations. Designed and built by BAE Systems each vessel has water jet propulsion allows high thrust at shallow draught. The combination of twin water jets and powerful diesel inboards gives all the craft good speed and range. All hull types have operating speeds in the range of 30 knots.

It can also be used as a general-purpose working boat in support of diving operations, ship-to-shore re-supply and inland water patrol. The boats are carried on a purpose-built launching and recovery trailer.

CHRIS MURKIN — HMC Protector

Border Force is a law enforcement command within the Home Office. Their official role is to secure the UK border by conducting immigration and customs controls for people and goods entering the UK. This rather generalised description of their role does not do the Border Force the justice it deserves. Additionally, Border Force is responsible for the collection of intelligence and for alerting the police and security services of suspicious activities, and for the searching of baggage, vehicles and cargo for illicit goods and illegal immigrants. In this role Border Force facilitates the legitimate movement of individuals and trade to and from the United Kingdom.

In the last decade, Border Force has been tasked with the unsavoury task of trying to stem the tide of illegal immigration across the English Channel. Often Border Force vessels appear in the media with their decks full of immigrants who have been rescued from the world's busiest seaway from their ill-equipped inflatable boats. In 2023, an estimated 30,000 people had attempted the hazardous crossing. That was a big drop from the 2022 total of 45,755, which was the highest number since figures began to be collected in 2018.

Border Force's responsibilities are not confined to the maritime environment as they are also responsible for airports, postal depots and railways, including Eurostar and Eurotunnel services at Folkestone. Border Force is split into five operational regions (Central, Heathrow, North, South and South-East and Europe).

• DEREK FOX HMC Seeker

BORDER FORCE
STAN PATROL 4207 CLASS

Vessel	Callsign	Completion Date	Builder
SEARCHER	ZQNK9	2002	Damen
SEEKER	ZQNL2	2001	Damen
VALIANT	MBLL8	2004	Damen
VIGILANT	ZITI4	2003	Damen

G.R.T.: 238 tonnes **Dimensions:** 42.8m x 7.11m x 2.52m **Machinery:** 2 Caterpillar 3516B diesels, 2 shafts; 2 4-blade controllable pitch propellors; 1 Promac bow thruster **Speed:** 26+ knots **Complement:** 12

Notes: These vessels are able to remain at sea for extended periods and in heavy weather conditions. They are mostly deployed on a risk-led or intelligence-led basis detecting prohibited and restricted goods, boarding and searching ships and providing a law enforcement presence in remote and inaccessible areas. Vessels are prefixed HMC for Her Majesty's Cutter. They were built at the Damen Shipyard in the Netherlands and all have a steel hull with an aluminium superstructure. All are based at Portsmouth and are normally not armed with fixed firearms, nor are crew armed. What is often taken to be a gun on the bow of the cutters is in fact a water hose. A 7m rigid inflatable boat (RIB) can be launched from the stern slipway.

HMC Protector

TELKKÄ CLASS

Vessel	Callsign	Completion Date	Builder
PROTECTOR	2GWY9	2002	UKI Workboat

Displacement: 434 tonnes **Dimensions:** 49.7m x 7.3m x 3.65m **Machinery:** 2 Wärtsilä 12V200 diesels, 7,240 hp; 2 shafts; CP propellor; bow and stern thrusters **Speed:** 22 knots **Complement:** 12

Notes: HMC PROTECTOR (not to be confused with HMS PROTECTOR) was acquired in August 2013 and commissioned in March 2014. She is the former Finnish Border Agency vessel TAVI. She replaced HMC SENTINEL which was retired in 2013. All HMC cutters operate 24 hours a day, 365 days per year, through the employment of dual crews. There are ten crews for the five Border Force cutters comprising 120 seagoing staff, working two weeks on and two weeks off.

Border Force also operate 10 Jet Ski's (known as Personal Water-Craft) equipped with rubberised fenders to prevent damaging their fibreglass skins when coming alongside vessels during boarding operations and 3 Rigid Inflatable Boats for a variety of tasks in sheltered inland waters around the coastline.

● GARRETT FULLER   HMC Hurricane

WINDFARM SUPPORT VESSELS

Vessel	Callsign	Completion Date	Builder
DEFENDER	---	2013	South Boats
RANGER	---	2014	South Boats
TYPHOON	---	2016	Aluminium Marine
HURRICANE	---	2016	Aluminium Marine

Displacement: 59 tonnes   **Dimensions:** 23m x 9m x 1.4m   **Machinery:** 2 x MTU 10V2000M72 and 2x Rolls Royce 56A3   **Speed:** 27 knots   **Complement:** 3

Notes: Until recently, the UK Border Force relied for Channel patrols mainly upon a fleet drawn from its inventory of five offshore patrol vessels backed up by six converted oil rig rescue craft deployed as coastal patrol craft. However, the fleet has been discreetly upgraded by the phased introduction of a flotilla of four chartered early-model catamaran craft that were formerly operated as windfarm support vessels (WFSVs). WFSVs were selected as they offer stability and increased carrying capacity. The introduction of these craft is the latest attempt to meet the challenge posed by mass irregular migration.

• DEREK FOX   HMC Speedwell

DELTA ARRC 190 CLASS

Vessel	Callsign	Completion Date	Builder
EAGLE	ZCPH5	2006	Holyhead Marine/Delta ARCC
NIMROD	2JQP9	2006	Holyhead Marine/Delta ARCC
ALERT	2JQQ2	2006	Holyhead Marine/Delta ARCC
ACTIVE	2JQQ3	2006	Holyhead Marine/Delta ARCC
HUNTER	ZCOO3	2006	Holyhead Marine/Delta ARCC
SPEEDWELL		2006	Holyhead Marine/Delta ARCC
ASTUTE		2006	Holyhead Marine/Delta ARCC
ARDENT		2006	Holyhead Marine/Delta ARCC

Displacement: 29 GRT **Dimensions:** 17.75m x 5.63m x 0.9m **Machinery:** 2 Caterpillar C18 diesels, 1,727 hp; 2 Hamilton waterjets **Speed:** 34 knots **Complement:** 6

Notes: Starting in 2016, to boost the number of vessels patrolling the UK coastline, eight ex-BP Project Jigsaw rescue craft, built by Holyhead Marine (Holyhead) and Delta ARCC (Stockport), were acquired by Border Force. They are termed Coastal Patrol Vessels within Border Force. As well as carrying out regular patrols of UK waters, CPVs will act on intelligence provided by law enforcement and international partners. Callsigns are displayed on the superstructure roof forward of the bridge. The design includes a deep-vee fibre-reinforced plastic hull design and can return to the upright position if capsized.

CROWN COPYRIGHT/MOD

n concert with virtually all the world's leading naval powers, the Royal Navy has had to reflect on the naval air wing of the future. What capabilities will be available and what sort of mix of manned and unmanned vehicles will comprise the air wing? Indeed, is there a role for manned aircraft in what has been named as Future Maritime Aviation Force (FMAF)?

Drones and unmanned aerial vehicles (UAVs) and a wide variety of other acronyms will dominate the vision for the Royal Navy and with a projected in-service timeline of 2030 the future is nearer than you think. The principal aim of FAMF is to increase the available mass, range, persistence and resilience of the Royal Navy airwing flying from the two Queen Elizabeth-class aircraft carriers, and with the use of small and medium sized Uncrewed Aerial Systems (UASs) virtually every ship, whatever it's displacement, could have some form of aerial component to its arsenal and available equipment by the end of this decade.

The introduction of new autonomous and digitally linked air vehicles will eventually possibly lead to the phasing out or supplementation of other older, more expensive and less reliable conventional and traditional systems and aircraft. New pilots entering the Royal Navy should not fear however, as the projected out-of-service timeframe for F-35B Lightning II aircraft is in the order of the 2050-60s. FAMF is primarily a Royal Navy project, but with the merging of F-35B Lightning II aircraft from the RN and RAF aboard aircraft carriers it is increasingly becoming a joint venture. Each service has technical insight, experience and ideas that will benefit the other mutually in their individual programmes.

One of the key words mentioned is mass. With fewer than 70 F-35B Lightning II strike aircraft available between the RN and RAF, there is clearly insufficient to satisfy all needs and to quickly replace battle damaged or lost aircraft in time of conflict. To create mass, there needs to be loads of aircraft – QED UAVs. Relatively simple, relatively cheap and easily mass produced, UAVs can act in 'swarms' given the right computer codes and instructions. The enemy defences could be swamped with targets allowing just enough to get through and attack, and all without risking the lives of aircrew. More sophisticated UAS are being developed that can act as tanker aircraft for manned and unmanned aerial vehicles whilst others are being developed with an ever increasingly complex suite of electronic sensors which can be placed in harms way but without the risks associated with manned aircraft. Such larger UAS may require specialist handling equipment on ships capable of operating them such as catapults and arrestor gear.

In the medium to long term, there is, however, no alternative than manned platforms in the skies over the oceans. The Human Eyeball No 1 is still one of the most advanced and sensitive sensors ever and will be hard to replicate. The centrepiece of Royal Navy maritime aviation will, for the next thirty-forty years, be the Lockheed Martin F-35B Lightning II Joint Strike Fighter. By 2027 the first 48 aircraft will have been delivered. The remainder of what is projected to be less than 80 in total will arrive in small numbers over the coming decades. It is likely that by 2030 the total available F-35Bs in the United Kingdom will be around 55 airframes. These aircraft will have been upgraded to take the latest weaponry including the SPEAR-3 standoff weapon and the Meteor BVRAAM. They will also have had Block 4 software upgrades installed. Currently the F-35B lacks a potent anti-ship/land attack missile but political deals are being made behind the scenes that could see the aircraft equipped with a suitable weapon as part of the FCASW programme, although the weapon systems will probably not materialise until around 2030.

The RN Merlin fleet's lifetime will be pushed out to until 2040 before replacements are purchased. This is a major ask because the Mk2s were expected to be retired in 2029 and the Mk4s (most recently refurbished) in 2030. The British defence budget has no available funding for replacement aircraft so the hope is continual upgrades of avionics and mission systems will suffice.

Wildcat has proven to be an agile, capable and lethal maritime helicopter and by 2030 it will have even more teeth with the installation of the Sea Venom missile in addition to the already operational Martlet missile. Not visible to the casual observer is the development of a new Tactical Data Link (TDL) for the Wildcat that will make the aircraft a much more effective anti-submarine warfare asset. Wildcats do, however, still lack a dipping sonar, a decision on the purchase of these is yet to be taken. By 2030 the Wildcat, it is hoped, will also mount the Future Lightweight Torpedo as a direct replacement for the Sting Ray which has been in service since the early 1980s.

Perhaps the most exciting and challenging current project will see the Royal Air Force and Royal Navy, and to a lesser extent the British Army, partner on Project VIXEN. For the Royal Navy this project could led to the reconfiguring of the flight decks of the two Queen Elizabeth-class aircraft carriers to include catapults and arresting gear for unmanned aerial vehicles (or drones). These so called 'loyal wingman' UAS will act as force multipliers for the F-35B Lightnings and could even potentially attack in swarms. These drones, if operated from the RN's carriers, could also perform the air-to-air refuelling (AAR) role in a similar fashion to the US Navy's MQ-25 Stingrays.

The biggest challenge of all for the Royal Navy's Future Maritime Aviation Force is how to achieve these lofty aims within the space of seven years. 2030 is closer than one thinks, and any hiccups or financial problems could easily upset the timescale. The challenge, however, is not solely on the shoulders of the military, it is being shared by industry and business partners who have a vested interest to make these systems and concepts succeed.

AIRCRAFT & UNITS

NAVY COMMAND SQUADRONS

809 NAS	Merlin HM2	TAG/RNAS Culdrose
814 NAS	Merlin HM2	TAG/RNAS Culdrose
815 NAS	Wildcat HMA2	Flights/RNAS Yeovilton
820 NAS	Merlin HM2	TAG/RNAS Culdrose
824 NAS	Merlin HM2	Training/RNAS Culdrose
825 NAS	Wildcat HMA2	Training/RNAS Yeovilton
849 NAS	Merlin HM2 'Crowsnest'	TAG/RNAS Culdrose
700X NAS		RNAS Culdrose
727 NAS	Tutor T1	Grading/RNAS Yeovilton
FOST Flight	Dauphin 2	HMNB Devonport

JOINT FORCE LIGHTNING

17 Sqn	F-35B Lightning II	Edwards AFB - USA
617 Sqn	F-35B Lightning II	TAG/RAF Marham
207 Sqn	F-35B Lightning II	Training/RAF Marham

JOINT HELICOPTER COMMAND

845 NAS	Merlin HC4/3i	TAG/RNAS Yeovilton
846 NAS	Merlin HC4/3i	TAG/RNAS Yeovilton
847 NAS	Wildcat AH1	TAG/RNAS Yeovilton
7 Sqn	Chinook HC4/4A/5	TAG/RAF Odiham
18 Sqn	Chinook HC4/4A/5	TAG/RAF Odiham
27 Sqn	Chinook HC4/4A/5	TAG/RAF Odiham
28(AC) Sqn	Chinook HC4/4A/5	Training/RAF Odiham
1 Regt.	Wildcat AH1	TAG/RNAS Yeovilton
3 Regt.	Apache AH1	TAG/AAC Wattisham
4 Regt.	Apache AH1	TAG/AAC Wattisham

MILITARY FLYING TRAINING SYSTEM

72(R) Sqn	Tucano T1	1 FTS/RAF Linton-on-Ouse
703 Sqn	Tutor T1	3 FTS/RAF Barkston Heath
750 NAS	Avenger T1	RNAS Culdrose
705 Sqn	Juno HT1	DHFS/RAF Shawbury

Training for pilots on the Hawk T1 have been halted due to engine problems. Therefore all references to Hawk T1 have been taken out.

British Warships & Auxiliaries 2024

• CROWN COPYRIGHT/MOD

Leonardo Helicopters MERLIN HM2

Role: Anti-submarine search and strike; maritime surveillance
Engines: 3 x Rolls Royce/Turbomeca RTM 322 each developing 2,100 shp
Length: 74' 10" **Rotor diameter:** 61' **Height:** 21' 10"
Max. Weight: 32,120lb **Max. Speed:** 167 knots **Crew:** 1/2 pilots, 1 observer, 1 aircrewman
Avionics: Blue Kestrel radar; Orange Reaper ESM; Folding Light Acoustic System for helicopters (FLASH); AQS-903 acoustic processor; Wescam MX-15 electro-optical/IR camera; defensive aids including Directional Infrared Countermeasures (DIRCM), AN/AAR-57 radar warning system, chaff and flare dispensers;
Armament: Up to 4 Stingray torpedoes or Mark 11 depth charges; 1 x M3M 0.5" machine-gun in cabin door and 1 x 7.62mm machine-gun in cabin window

Squadron Service: 814, 820, 824, 849 Naval Air Squadrons

Notes: 814 NAS is the biggest Merlin Mk2 helicopter Squadron that the Royal Navy ever had (it merged with the decommissioned 829 Naval Air Squadron at the end of March 2018). The merger might signal the start of the execution of the MoD forward plan which shows 820 NAS allocated for carrier embarkation between 2018-2026 and 814 (and now 829) NAS specialising in providing aircraft for RFAs and frigates. 824 NAS is the training unit for all anti-submarine aircrew, ASaC 'Crowsnest' and commando Merlin pilots. 'Crowsnest' fitted Merlins, in which anti-submarine role equipment can be replaced by ASaC sensors and consoles, are being delivered by Leonardo helicopters. ASaC observer training will be carried out by the HQ Flight of 849 NAS and operational aircraft were allocated to TAGs in 2021. The Merlin Mk2, as part of the the Crowsnest programme, has replaced the Navy's Sea King Mk7 Airborne Surveillance and Control of 849 Naval Air Squadron (now retired) – and like their predecessors will be based at Royal Naval Air Station Culdrose, which also provides anti-submarine Merlin aircraft to protect the Fleet.

NAVY COMMAND

Crowsnest

Crowsnest is the name given to the Merlin Helicopters fitted with a large inflatable radome commonly known as 'baggers' in the Royal Navy. These helicopters provide airborne aerial surveillance and the control of other aircraft (known as ASAC). Inside the radome is the Lockheed Martin Searchwater Radar that, from its airborne position, can detect threats well in advance of shipborne sensors and increase the reaction time of the ships defences and complement. In the 1950s and until 1978 with the withdrawal of the last British conventional aircraft carrier ARK ROYAL the role was performed by Fairey Gannet AEW aircraft and then following the Falklands War of 1982 by Sea Kings of 849 Naval Air Squadron. With the withdrawal of the Sea Kings from service the role passed to the Merlin equipped Fleet Air Arm.

Crowsnest has experienced a troubled development programme. The contract with Lockheed Martin was placed in 2016, who subcontracted the work to Thales and Leonardo Helicopters. The high-risk programme quickly fell behind and scheduled milestones were routinely being missed. The IOC (initial operating capability) slipped 18 months to September 2021, four months after QUEEN ELIZABETH sailed on her historic first operational deployment to the Far East. Some elements of Crowsnest were available for the deployment but not the complete required package that linked the Searchwater Radar with the Cerberus mission system. The latest IOC issued by the MoD is for some time in 2023 with full operational capability to be declared some time later.

Such is the pace of technological innovation and development there is already talk of Crowsnest's possible future replacement. The Royal Air Force is at the early stages of

developing the ALVINA swarming drone for use with its fleet of Typhoon and F-35B jet fighters. These swarms will operate to act as decoys, distraction and electronic jamming roles in contested aerial environments. It is likely similar systems will be proposed for Project PROTEUS, a plan to develop a mid-sized RWAS capable of carrier operation and hunting submarines via sonobuoy and dipping sonar, in addition to providing a replacement for Crowsnest in the longer term. The RWAS will also contribute to the Maritime Intra-Theatre Lift (MITL).

By 2029 Project PROTEUS is projected to have matured sufficiently to release 'the expensive to operate' Merlin fleet from Crowsnest duties and allow them to concentrate on tracking and attacking enemy submarines. There have, however, been doubts raised about how such a system could be developed in the space of just 5 years given the developmental history of the Crowsnest system.

CROWN COPYRIGHT/MOD

Leonardo Helicopters WILDCAT HMA2

Roles: Surface search and strike; anti-submarine strike; boarding party support
Engines: 2 x LHTEC CTS 800 each developing 1,362 shp
Length: 50' **Rotor diameter:** 42' **Height:** 12'
Max. Weight: 13,200lb **Max. Speed:** 157 knots **Crew:** 1 pilot & 1 observer
Avionics: Selex-Galileo Sea Spray 7400E multi-mode AESA radar; Wescam MX-15 electro-optical/IR camera; Electronic warfare system and defensive aids suite. Bowman communications system
Armament: 2 x Stingray torpedoes or Mark 11 depth charges; 1 x M3M 0.5" machine-gun in cabin door. From 2020 to carry Martlet (light) and Sea Venom (heavy) air-to-surface guided weapons.

Squadron Service: 815, 825 Naval Air Squadrons

Notes: 825 NAS is the training and tactical development unit and 815 NAS deploys flights of 1 or 2 aircraft to destroyers, frigates and some RFAs that do not embark Merlins. Wildcat is designed around a digital avionics management system that enhances mission effectiveness and reduces aircrew workload. Its 'paperless' maintenance system is shared with the Wildcat AH 1 operated by the Joint Helicopter Command. With the Lynx HMA 8 withdrawn from service in 2017, Wildcats now fully equip these two naval air squadrons which are both shore-based at RNAS Yeovilton. The HMA 2 has a significant strike capability since the Martlet and Sea Venom air-to-surface guided weapons achieved initial operational capability. Each Wildcat helicopter is capable of carrying 20 Martlett missiles. With the withdrawal from service of 700X NAS ScanEagle detachments in 2017, Wildcats and Merlins are the only air assets capable of deployment in destroyers, frigates and RFAs. In October 2021, HMS DEFENDER'S Wildcat helicopter from 815 Naval Air Squadron fired a Martlet missile – the first time the lightweight missile has been fired by the Royal Navy on frontline operations.

• CROWN COPYRIGHT/MOD

Leonardo Helicopters WILDCAT AH1

Role: Battlefield reconnaissance; airborne command and control, force protection and troop transport.
Engines: 2 x LHTEC CTS 800-4N turboshafts each developing 1,362 shp
Length: 50'   **Rotor diameter:** 42'   **Height:** 12'
Max. Weight: 13,200lb   **Max. Speed:** 157 knots   **Crew:** 2 pilots & 1 gunner
Avionics: L-3 Wescam MX-15Di electro-optical/laser designator turret; digital mission planning system; Selex HIDAS 15 electronic warfare system
Armament: Door-mounted 0.5 inch M3M machine gun.

Squadron Service: 847 Naval Air Squadron, 1 Regiment Army Air Corps

Notes: 847 NAS is shore-based at RNAS Yeovilton and operates the Wildcat AH 1 as part of the Commando Helicopter Force, within the Joint Helicopter Command, to support 3 Commando Brigade with battlefield reconnaissance and airborne command and control of forces on the ground. 1 Regiment is also based at RNAS Yeovilton and operates, effectively, as a joint force with the RN Wildcat squadrons. It comprises a headquarters squadron plus 652, 659 and 661 Squadrons which operate their Wildcats as a specialised intelligence, surveillance and reconnaissance aircraft in support of troops on the ground. In the troop-lift role, Army Wildcats can lift up to 5 fully-equipped troops over short distances. Like 847 NAS they can be embarked to form part of a TAG when required and AAC pilots are trained to operate from the sea.

• CROWN COPYRIGHT/MOD

Lockheed Martin F-35B LIGHTNING II

Role: Strike, fighter and reconnaissance aircraft
Engine: 1 X Pratt & Whitney F135-PW-600 delivering 41,000lb thrust with reheat in conventional flight; 40,650lb hover thrust with Rolls-Royce lift fan engaged and tail nozzle rotated.
Length: 51' 4"   **Wingspan:** 35'   **Height:** 15'
Max. Weight: 60,000lb **Max. Speed:** Mach 1.6 **Crew:** 1 pilot
Avionics: AN/APG-81 AESA radar; AN/AAQ-40 electro-optical targeting system; AN/AAQ-37 distributed aperture system; AN/ASQ-239 'Barracuda' electronic warfare system; pilot's helmet-mounted display system; multi-function advanced data link.
Armament: Current Block 2B software allows the stealthy carriage of weapons in 2 internal bays with a single ASRAAM or AMRAAM air-to-air missile plus a single 1,000lb bomb equivalent such as Paveway IV LGB in each. Block 3F software in operational aircraft delivered from 2017 will enable the additional use of 7 non-stealthy external pylons, 3 under each wing and 1 under the centreline. A total of 12,000lb of weapons or fuel tanks to be carried; inner wing pylons have 'plumbing' for 426 US gallon drop tanks.

Squadron Service: 17, 207, 617 Squadrons.

Notes: The F-35B Lightning II Joint Strike Fighter is a multi-national Fifth Generation fighter aircraft that provides the Royal Navy with its fleet defence and strike capability operating from the Queen Elizabeth-class aircraft carriers. Britain is the sole Tier One Country alongside the Americans, and over 25,000 British jobs are dependent upon the programme. It also injects around £35 billion into the British economy. Originally, the MoD committed to purchasing a total of 138 F-35B Lightnings from Lockheed Martin over the lifetime of the programme which would have been delivered in batches. This number has, however, been whittled down until now the RN/RAF will receive just 48 examples of the type. This number is somewhat misleading as three of the British aircraft are test examples that are based in the United States and will never leave the USA.

JOINT FORCE LIGHTNING

The UK received six F-35Bs in 2022 and a further seven were due to be delivered in 2023. The schedule after these dates was uncertain following a temporary shutdown in production at Lockheed Martin after the discovery that a critical component in the aircraft's construction was being sourced from China.

The F-35Bs are jointly operated by the Fleet Air Arm and the Royal Air Force. Towards the end of 2023 Royal Navy 809 Naval Air Squadron stood up for service. 809 Naval Air Squadron has an illustrious history having been involved in the invasions of North Africa, Italy and Southern France during World War 2 and later in November 1956 saw active service during Operation Musketeer during the Suez Crisis. After flying from the decks of the aircraft carriers HERMES and INVINCIBLE in the Falklands War the squadron was disbanded 17 December 1982.

CROWN COPYRIGHT/MOD   F-35B

What is the cowling right behind the cockpit used for?
The F-35B short takeoff and vertical landing (STOVL) capabilities are made possible through the Rolls-Royce patented shaft-driven LiftFan propulsion system installed behind the jet's cockpit, and an engine that can swivel 90 degrees when in short takeoff/vertical landing mode. When the jet is set to 'Lift' mode two doors open behind the cockpit, one being the cowling for the air intake for the 50-inch titanium LiftFan. The cowling opens only when hovering, short take-offs, or landing vertically. It directs air down into the LiftFan and closes during normal flight covering the lift fan. The smaller doors behind the big cowling gives additional clean air to the engine which is operating high during this time.

• CROWN COPYRIGHT/MOD

Leonardo Helicopters MERLIN HC3, HC3i, HC4

Role: Commando assault, load-lifting, troop movement
Engines: 3 x Rolls Royce/Turbomeca RTM 322 each developing 2,100 shp
Length: 74' 10" **Rotor diameter:** 61' **Height:** 21' 10"
Max. Weight: 32,120lb **Max. Speed:** 167 knots **Crew:** 1 or 2 pilots, 1 aircrewman
Avionics: Wescam MX-15 electro-optical/IR camera; defensive aids suite including directional IR countermeasures, AN/AAR-57 missile approach warning system, automatic chaff and flare dispensers
Armament: 1 x M3M 0.5" machine-gun in cabin door; 1 x 7.62mm machine-gun in cabin window

Squadron Service: 845, 846 Naval Air squadrons.

Notes: The first of 25 Merlin HC3s to be modified to HC4 standard was delivered by Leonardo Helicopters in 2017 and the last was due to be delivered in 2020, restoring an embarked capability to the Commando Helicopter Force, CHF. 7 aircraft have been modified to an interim HC3i standard to give some TAG capability until sufficient HC4s are available. The HC4 has a 'glass cockpit' similar to that of the HM2, power-folding main rotor head and tail pylon together with improved communications and defensive aids. Unlike the green HC3s, Merlin HC4s are painted grey. 845 NAS is eventually to have 10 aircraft deployable in up to 3 TAGs and 846 NAS is also to have 10 with an operational conversion/training flight, a maritime counter-terrorism flight and, after 2020, a TAG flight to back up 845. The remaining 5 airframes give deep maintenance flexibility and will act as attrition reserves.

The Merlin helicopter does not have the capability to lift and transport a jet engine for the F-35 which causes issues at the MoD. Due to funding constraints the MoD does not have a solution despite the Maritime Intra-theatre Lift Capability requiring the need to move people and equipment, especially parts for the F-35.

JOINT HELICOPTER COMMAND

• CROWN COPYRIGHT/MOD

Leonardo Helicopters APACHE AH1

Role: Attack and armed reconnaissance helicopter
Engines: 2 x Rolls Royce/Turbomeca RTM 322 turboshafts each developing 2,100 shp
Length: 58' 3" **Rotor diameter:** 48' **Height:** 15' 3"
Max. Weight: 15,075lb **Max. Speed:** 150 knots **Crew:** 2 pilots
Avionics: Selex HIDAS defensive aids suite; Longbow radar; optical and infrared target indication sensors.
Armament: Up to 16 AGM-114 Hellfire air-to-surface guided weapons; up to 4 Sidewinder air-to-air missiles; M230 30mm cannon with 1,160 rounds; up to 76 CRV-7 unguided air-to-surface missiles.

Squadron Service: 3 and 4 Regiments Army Air Corps

Notes: 3 Regiment AAC comprises 653, 662 and 663 Squadrons. 4 Regiment comprises 656 and 664 Squadrons and both formations are based at the AAC base at RAF Wattisham and form part of the Joint Helicopter Command. Apaches of 656 Squadron flew successfully on operations over Libya with a TAG embarked in OCEAN during 2011 and at least one unit is maintained at high readiness for embarked operations as part of a TAG but in an emergency a larger number of Apaches could be embarked if required.

The Apache AH1 is to reach its out-of-service date in 2024 and be replaced by the Boeing AH-64D Apache Longbow attack helicopter. In 2021 the MoD decided on the weaponry for the Army Apache which can operate from the Navy's two carriers. The Lockheed Martin AGM-179 joint air-to-ground missile has been selected. Apache will also be equipped with Hellfire K-1 and Romeo missiles.

• CROWN COPYRIGHT/MOD

Boeing CHINOOK HC4, HC4A and HC5

Role: Battlefield transport helicopter
Engines: 2 x Avco Lycoming T55-L-712 turboshafts each developing 3,750 shp
Length: 98' 9" **Rotor diameter:** 60' **Height:** 18' 8"
Max. weight: 50,000lb **Max. speed:** 160 knots **Crew:** 2 pilots & 2 aircrewmen/gunners
Avionics: Infrared jammer; missile warning system; integrated digital 'glass cockpit'; moving map tablet and improved crewman's work station.
Armament: up to 2 M 134 mini guns mounted in doorways; one M 60 machine gun on rear loading ramp.

Squadron Service: 7, 18, 27, 28(AC) Squadrons Royal Air Force

Notes: All 4 squadrons are based at RAF Odiham from where the 3 operational units can provide TAG detachments when required. The Chinook's rotor blades cannot fold but QUEEN ELIZABETH's side lifts are large enough to strike down the aircraft, fully spread, into the hangar and they can be embarked in significant numbers to support both amphibious, military and humanitarian operations. Chinooks can carry 54 fully-equipped troops, 24 stretcher cases or loads up to 44,000lb carried both internally and externally over short distances. With extra fuel tanks they have a range of 1,000nm with a light load. Originally designed for the US Army, Chinooks are in widespread service throughout the world. The Boeing Chinook Helicopter entered service on the 22nd November 1980. Throughout its 40+ years of service the Chinook has made an immeasurable contribution to the Service, supporting communities across the UK and operating in every major conflict since the Falklands War.

SCHIEBEL S-100 CAMCAMPTOR

Role: Situational awareness and reconnaissancee
Wingspan: 3.4m **Weight:** 110kg **Top speed:** 222kph
Range: 180 miles **Armament:** None
Squadron Service: 700X Naval Air Squadron

Notes: On 10 February 2023 it was announced that the Royal Navy had selected Thales and Schiebel to provide a new rotary-wing Unmanned Aerial Vehicle (UAS) for use on board Type 23 frigates under the terms of its Peregrine programme. Previously known as the Flexible Tactical Uncrewed Air System (FTUAS), Peregrine will see the Schiebel S-100 Camcopter equipped with a Thales I-Master radar to act as an additional eye in the sky to enhance the situational awareness of deployed Type 23 frigates. The system was selected as an urgent capability requirement.

AEROVIRONMENT RQ-20 PUMA

Role: Survey and reconnaissance **Length:** 4.6ft (1.4m) **Wingspan:** 9.2ft (2.8m)
Weight: 14lb (6.3kg) **Endurance:** 3+ hours and 15 miles range **Armament:** None
Squadron Service: 700X Naval Air Squadron

Notes: This hand launched drone is being operated by 700X Naval Air Squadron from its base at RNAS Culdrose whose role is to develop a strategy, resources and training within the Royal Navy to deploy these aircraft in the future. To this end they run two different courses, the first which is run 10 times annually instructs 150 personnel in the use of drones generally. The second course is dedicated to those personnel who will operate the RQ-20 PUMA. Puma AE (All Environment) is a fully waterproof, small, unmanned aircraft system (UAS) designed for land and maritime operations. Capable of landing in water or on land, the Puma AE empowers the operator with an operational flexibility never before available in the small UAS class. The enhanced precision navigation system with secondary GPS provides greater positional accuracy and reliability. AV's common ground control system allows the operator to control the aircraft manually or programme it for GPS based autonomous navigation.

EVOLVE DYNAMIC'S SKY MANTIS

Role: Survey and reconnaissance **Engines:** 4 x Electric Motors **Armament:** None
Squadron Service: 700X Naval Air Squadron

Notes: Described as a Rapid Response/Deployment Medium Size Multi Rotor Surveillance & Special Mission drone, the Evolve Dynamics' Sky Mantis can operate in a variety of weather conditions including heavy rain and windspeeds up to 75 km/h (46 mph or 40 knots). The drone carries a Dual HD 30X zoom low light EO and 640x512 30FPS thermal imaging camera as standard. The system, the manufacturers claim, can be operational within 1 minute and can fly for 1 hour with onboard battery power. The payload of the drone can be customisable for photography, mapping, survey and even gas sniffer roles. The Sky Mantis has been extensively tested on board HMS PROTECTOR.

PROJECT VIXEN

The VIXEN project represents a cutting-edge Uncrewed Aerial System (UAS) and is one of the most complex projects of its type. It is not expected to reach fruition until the 2030s but will deliver a fixed-wing air vehicle capable of accommodating two 500kg payloads. It will be of considerable size and would require a suitable catapult arrangement to be installed on board both HMS PRINCE OF WALES and HMS QUEEN ELIZABETH to operate at sea. This is not as big a problem as it might at first appear as both aircraft carriers were designed for, but not with, catapults as they were being built. Project ARK ROYAL is a Royal Navy programme currently investigating the possibility of installing catapults on the two carriers. These catapults range widely in size, cost and complexity. VIXEN will offer the Royal Navy an enhanced control of a wider battlespace around each carrier and could be used in support of Persistent Wide Area Surveillance, Electronic Warfare (EW) and, eventually, armed strike missions.

Like most post-war British aviation projects VIXEN's development has been torturous having started as an RAF project (Mosquito UAS) before being abandoned in June 2022. Recently interest has shifted towards the MQ-28 Ghost Bat UAS under development by American aviation giant Boeing on behalf of the Australian Air Force. With deeper and growing tri-partite defence agreements (including AUKUS submarines) between the United States, Australia and the UK, further development of this system is extremely likely, although other options exist with the American XQ-58 Valkyrie (used by US Marines), the Turkish Bayraktar Kizilelma and another collaborative effort between Italy and Japan all being potential future programme partners.

PROJECT PROTEUS

In September 2023, at the DSEI exhibition held in London, Leonardo and the British MoD showcased a new innovative drone concept that is intended to join the fleet in the coming years and relieve the Merlin fleet of many of its more onerous roles and allowing them to concentrate on anti-submarine warfare. PROTEUS has been under development under the terms of Phase3a the Rotary Wing Uncrewed Air System (RWUAS) Technology Demonstrator Programme (TDP).

The single engined aircraft is in the 2-3 tonnes range and will add significantly to what has been dubbed 'conceptual maturity' of the airframe, avionics and integrated system hardware and software. Proteus is expected to make its first flight around 2025 and will, when in service, lead future development of similar progressively more capable unmanned aerial systems. PROTEUS is projected to work alongside the existing Merlin Mk2s and in some instances replace them, particularly in secondary roles such as transportation of goods and supplies. Each airframe will have 2 x 500kg modular payload capacity and may even be sufficiently powerful to lift an ASaC radar system. If successful future iterations of PROTEUS could also be weaponised for ASW roles armed potentially with depth charges and bombs. PROTEUS will also be small and flexible enough to be carried by a wider range of naval vessels than is currently possible with the Wildcat and Merlin fleets.

PROJECT VAMPIRE

When the RAFs' Hawk T1 training aircraft were retired in March 2022 it left the Royal Navy without any fast jet adversary training aircraft. VAMPIRE is planned to provide a partial replacement for the Hawk jets with a relatively simple fixed-wing Unmanned Aerial System. Each drone would be fitted with a variety of payloads that can simulate battlespace environments including radar and cameras as well as more complex technology for use during Cyber and Electro-magnetic Activities (CEMA), Electronic Warfare (EW) and also for decoy purposes. It is proposed that VAMPIRE will use the tried and tested Qinetiq Banshee target drone as a basis for development. It has also been suggested that the long range of the drone could be utilised as a submarine detector if it were equipped with a Magnetic Anomaly detector in addition to the RAF's fleet of P-8A Poseidon maritime patrol aircraft.

PROJECT PANTHER

The Royal Navy has initiated an industry-wide competition under the terms of the Uncrewed Aerial System Heavy Lift Challenge (UASHLC) programme to develop and deliver to the fleet an innovative Logistics Uncrewed Aerial System (UAS) for ship-to-ship and ship-to-shore operations. This vital mission will include beyond visual line of sight operations, currently something that drone technology sometimes struggles with achieving. Given the name PANTHER the new programme will see any aircraft given capabilities to transport various essential items, ranging from munitions and food to medicines and spare parts. The programme will, if completely achieved, revolutionise the way in which deployed vessels receive supplies as it will reduce the need for manned aircraft to be used at much greater cost.

Industry has already stepped up to the initial starting block for the programme with potential competitors, Malloy Aeronautics T-600 quadcopter and Windracer Ultra fixed wing drones being frontrunners at this early stage in the programme. In October 2023 HMS PRINCE OF WALES became the first carrier to receive on board a fixed wing conventional landing drone onto its flight deck.

• CROWN COPYRIGHT/MOD   HMS Prince of Wales

Military Flying Training System

CROWN COPYRIGHT/MOD

• CROWN COPYRIGHT/MOD

BAE Systems HAWK T2

Role: Advanced fast-jet training aircraft for RAF, RN and RM pilots
Engine: 1 x Rolls Royce Adour 951 FADEC/turbofan delivering 6,500lb of thrust
Length: 41' **Wingspan:** 32' 7" **Height:** 13' 1"
Max. Weight: 20,000lb **Max. Speed:** Mach 1 at altitude **Crew:** 1 or 2 pilots
Avionics: Two mission computers host simulations of sensor and weapons systems; a data link allows synthetic radar inputs for intercept training and synthetic electronic warfare threats. Inertial and GPS navigation systems.
Armament: 7 hardpoints capable of carrying a total of 6,800lb of weapons, including 1 x 30mm cannon pod on centreline, AIM-9 Sidewinder or ASRAAM missiles and bombs.

Squadron Service: 100 Squadron RAF

Notes: 4 (Reserve) Squadron forms part of Number 4 Flying Training School at RAF Valley within the Military Flying Training System and provides advanced fast-jet training for RAF, RN and RM pilots up to the standard required for conversion onto operational types. The Hawk T 2 has a 'glass cockpit' with 3 full-colour, multi-function displays, similar to those in the Typhoon and F-35B, which display navigation, weapons and system information intended to immerse student pilots into a complex, data-rich tactical flying environment from the outset rather than just learning to fly the aircraft.

In October 2021, 736 NAS was disbanded due to the retirement of the Hawk T1 and 100 Squadron RAF assumed maritime training support flying the Hawk T Mark II.

• CROWN COPYRIGHT/MOD

Short TUCANO T1

Role: Basic fast-jet training aircraft for RAF, RN and RM pilots
Engine: 1 x Garrett TPE 331-12B turboprop delivering 1,100 shp
Length: 32' 4" **Wingspan:** 37' **Height** 11' 2"
Max. Weight: 7,220lb   **Max. Speed:** 300 knots **Crew:** 1 or 2 pilots
Avionics: Standard communications fit
Armament: None

Squadron Service 72(R) Squadron Royal Air Force

Notes: Operated by 72 (Reserve) Squadron as part of Number 1 Flying Training School at RAF Linton-on-Ouse, an element of the Military Flying Training System, the Tucano provides basic training for student RAF, RN and RM fast-jet pilots and RAF weapons system operators; it handles like a jet aircraft but is significantly cheaper to operate. Plans to replace the Tucano with the Beechcraft T-6C Texan II in 2019 have been delayed.

• CROWN COPYRIGHT/MOD

Grob TUTOR T1

Role: Elementary training
Engine: 1 x Textron Lycoming AE10-360-B1F developing 180 hp
Length: 24' 9" **Wingspan:** 32' 9" **Height:** 7'
Max. Weight: 2,178lb **Max. Speed:** 185 knots **Crew:** 2 pilots
Avionics: None
Armament: None

Squadron Service: 727 Naval Air Squadron, 703 Squadron MFTS

Notes: Tutors are used within Navy Command for the grading of potential aircrew and, in the short term, to clear a backlog in the MFTS. They provide elementary flying training for up to 12 student pilots per year. 703 Squadron is not a naval air squadron although it is numbered in what was until recently an exclusively naval sequence. It is part of the MFTS, providing elementary pilot training at RAF Barkston Heath for RN and RM pilots and Phase 1 and 2 training for RN observers. The aircraft is constructed mainly from carbon fibre reinforced plastic, which combines high strength with light weight. It has side-by-side seating with the primary flight instruments on the right-hand side of the cockpit. Thus, the student flies the aircraft from the right-hand seat with a right-hand stick and a left-hand throttle making transition to operational aircraft easier.

CROWN COPYRIGHT/MOD

Beech AVENGER T1

Role: Observer training
Engines: 2 x Pratt & Whitney PT6A-60A, each developing 1,050 shp
Length: 46' 8" **Wingspan:** 57' 11" **Height:** 14' 4"
Max. Weight: 15,000lb **Max. Speed;** 313 knots
Crew: 1 or 2 pilots, 4 student observers plus instructors
Avionics: Surface search and ground mapping radar
Armament: None

Squadron Service: 750 Naval Air Squadron

Notes: Avengers are civil-owned but military registered and used by 750 NAS at RNAS Culdrose as part of the MFTS. They provide Phase 3 training for RN observers and lead-in training for RAF AWACS systems operators. Phases 1 and 2 of the Observer Course are carried out by 703 Squadron at RAF Barkston Heath.

Airbus JUNO HT1

Role: Basic helicopter training
Engines: 2 x Turbomeca Arrius 2B, each developing 708 shp
Length: 39' 7" **Rotor diameter:** 33' 5" **Height:** 12' 4"
Max. Weight: 6,570lb **Max. Speed:** 140 knots
Crew: 2 pilots plus up to 6 passengers
Avionics: Defensive aids simulator; L-3 Wescam electro/optical camera
Armament: None

Squadron Service: 705 Squadron MFTS

Notes: The Juno HT1 began flying training at the Defence Helicopter School at RAF Shawbury in April 2018, replacing the Squirrel HT1. With twin engines and a night-vision goggle compatible glass cockpit, the helicopter gives student pilots a better lead-in to operational types such as the Merlin and Wildcat than its predecessors. All 29 Junos are fitted with a defensive aids simulator operated by the instructor and wired for an electro/optical camera installation although at any one time only 10 will be so fitted with the aim of teaching students to operate, rather than just fly modern aircraft types.

• CROWN COPYRIGHT/MOD

Eurocopter AS365N DAUPHIN 2

Role: Passenger movement and training support
Engines: 2 x Turbomeca Arriel 2C each developing 838 shp
Length: 39' 9" **Rotor diameter:** 39' 2" **Height:** 13' 4"
Max. Weight: 9,480lb **Max. Speed:** 155 knots **Crew:** 1 or 2 pilots plus up to 11 passengers
Avionics: None
Armament: None

Notes: Similar to the H-65 helicopters operated by the US Coast Guard, 2 of these civil-owned military-registered, COMR, helicopters are operated for the RN by Babcock Mission Critical Services Offshore Limited (known as Bond Offshore Helicopters until 25 April 2016) under contract. They are maintained at Newquay airport and used to support FOST in the sea areas off Plymouth. They are commonly tasked to transfer passengers between ships at sea but can also undertake a wide variety of other roles. On a day-to-day basis they fly from an operating facility within Devonport Naval base from which FOST staff can be flown from their headquarters directly to ships at sea.

Babcock operates a mixed fleet of helicopters on behalf of more than 10 major customers, specialising in providing offshore helicopter transportation services to North Sea and Irish Sea oil and gas platforms.

CROWN COPYRIGHT/MOD

Sea Launched Missiles

Trident II D5

The American built Lockheed Martin Trident 2 (D5) submarine launched strategic missiles are Britain's only nuclear weapons and form the UK contribution to the NATO strategic deterrent. 16 missiles, each capable of carrying up to 6 UK manufactured thermonuclear warheads (but currently limited to 4 under current government policy), can be carried aboard each of the Vanguard-class SSBNs. Trident has a maximum range of 12,000 km and is powered by a three stage rocket motor. Launch weight is 60 tonnes, overall length and width are 13.4 metres and 2.1 metres respectively.

Tomahawk (BGM-109)

This is a land attack cruise missile with a range of 1600 km and can be launched from a variety of platforms including surface ships and submarines. Some 65 of the latter version were purchased from America to arm Trafalgar-class SSNs with the first being delivered to the Royal Navy for trials during 1998. Tomahawk is fired in a disposal container from the submarine's conventional torpedo tubes and is then accelerated to its subsonic cruising speed by a booster rocket motor before a lightweight F-107 turbojet takes over for the cruise. Its extremely accurate guidance system means that small targets can be hit with precision at maximum range, as was dramatically illustrated in the Gulf War and Afghanistan. Total weight of the submarine version, including its launch capsule is 1816 kg, it carries a 450 kg warhead, length is 6.4 metres and wingspan (fully extended) 2.54 m. Fitted in Astute & T-class submarines. It was announced in 2014 that the US Navy are to stop procuring the missile in 2015 which has implications for the production line, although an MoD spokesman expected this not to impact on UK requirements.

Harpoon

The Harpoon is a sophisticated surface-to-surface missile using a combination of inertial guidance and active radar homing to attack targets out to a range of 130 km, cruising at Mach 0.9 and carrying a 227 kg warhead. It is powered by a lightweight turbojet but is accelerated at launch by a booster rocket. Fitted to Type 23 frigates and four Type 45 destroyers. Harpoon was planned to be retired from Royal Navy service at the end of 2018, but this was extended to 2023. The future anti-ship missile system, a joint UK/French programme, will not be in service until 2030 at the very earliest.

Naval Strike Missile

For well over three decades the main long range striking weapon of the Royal Navy's surface fleet was the American Harpoon anti-ship missile. The current inventory of this weapon, however, is fast approaching its out-of-service date which had left a major hole in the Royal Navy's offensive strike capability. The Ministry of Defence (MoD) however has secured a deal with the Norwegian arms manufacturer Kongsberg Defence and Aerospace to acquire the Naval Strike Missile (NSM) which has been put into service with several other NATO navies including the US Navy. The NSM is a long range (greater than 100 nautical miles) anti-ship missile and carries a 500 pound class warhead with a programmable fuze. The missiles are capable of evading enemy defences and fly at sea-skimming level. The missiles are being rushed into service and will be fitted to 11 Type 23 frigates and all six Type 45 destroyers.

Sea Viper (Aster 15/30)

Two versions of the Aster missile equip the Type 45 Destroyer, the shorter range Aster 15 and the longer range Aster 30. The missiles form the weapon component of the Principal Anti Air Missile System (PAAMS). Housed in a 48 cell Sylver Vertical Launch system, the missile mix can be loaded to match the ships requirement. Aster 15 has a range of 30 km while Aster 30 can achieve 100 km. The prime external difference between the two is the size of the booster rocket attached to the bottom of the missile. PAAMS is known as Sea Viper in RN service.

In December 2022 the UK Government joined representatives of France and Italy and signed an agreement to develop the Aster 30 missile into a maritime ballistic defence variant. The UK's stock of missiles will be converted to the Aster 30 B1 Naval UK standard which will see further enhancements of the autopilot software and logistical updates. The work will be carried out at Defence Munitions, Gosport

Sea Wolf

Short range rapid reaction anti-missile and anti-aircraft weapon. The complete weapon system, including radars and fire control computers, is entirely automatic in operation. Type 23 frigates carry 32 Vertical Launch Sea Wolf (VLS) in a silo on the foredeck. Basic missile data: weight 82 kg, length 1.9 m, wingspan 56 cm, range c.5-6 km, warhead 13.4 kg. The VLS missile is basically similar but has jettisonable tandem boost rocket motors. The Sea Wolf system is gradually being replaced by Sea Ceptor.

Sea Ceptor

Incorporating the Common Anti-Air Modular Missile (CAMM) family, being developed to replace the Rapier and Sea Wolf SAM systems, plus the ASRAAM short range Air-to-Air Missile. It will arm the Royal Navy's Type 23 frigates and its Type 26 Global Combat Ships. In Spring 2012 the MoD awarded MBDA UK a five-year Demonstration Phase contract worth £483 million to develop the missile for the RN. In September 2013 a £250 million contract was announced to manufacture the missile in the UK, sustaining around 250 jobs at MBDA sites in Stevenage, Filton and Lostock. Installation of the Sea Ceptor on Type 23 frigates started in 2015 with ARGYLL and the last one was scheduled to be completed by 2021 but this has now been delayed. CAMM missiles will be fitted in the existing VL Sea Wolf silo (one canister per cell for a maximum of 32 missiles).

The first Sea Ceptor-enhanced Type 45 is expected to be delivered by the summer of 2026 with the entire flotilla completed by winter 2032. That is six ships updated over a six-year period.

Sea Venom

Formerly known as the Future Anti-Surface Guided Weapon (Heavy), Sea Venom is a high-subsonic 'drop-launch' missile in the 110 kg-class incorporating an imaging infrared seeker (with provisions for an additional semi-active laser guidance channel), a two-way datalink for operator-in-the-loop control, and a 30kg warhead. Designed by MBDA to replace the helicopter air-launched Exocet, the missile will have a range of up to 25 km and will be able to counter targets up to corvette size. The FASGW programme, comprising both Heavy and Light missiles, is a joint venture between the UK and France. The missile will equip the RNs Wildcat helicopter. In July 2014, AgustaWestland received a £90 million contract to integrate the respective variants for deployment from the Wildcat HMA2. Each aircraft will be able to carry four missiles and Initial Operating Capability was achieved in 2020.

Martlet

Formerly known as the Future Anti-Surface Guided Weapon (Light), this missile is designed to counter small boat and fast inshore attack craft threats. It is based on the laser beam-riding variant of the Thales Lightweight Multi-role Missile (LMM). With a range of up to 8 km it carries a 3 kg blast fragmentation/shaped charge warhead travelling at about Mach 1.5. Missiles will be carried in a five-round launcher (with each Wildcat able to carry up to four launchers). Alternatively a mix of two Sea Venom on the outer pylon and two five round Martlet on the inner weapons station can be carried. An active laser guidance unit integrated within the L-3 Wescam nose turret will support laser beam-riding guidance.

Guns

BAE 127mm (5") 62 calibre (Mk45) lightweight gun

Used by the US Navy in various calibres since 1953 this 5-inch gun mount will be installed on the Type 26 frigates. Originally designed and built by United Defense in the United States, until that company was bought by BAE Systems Land & Armaments in June 2005. The Royal Navy version consists of a longer-barrel L62 Mark 36 gun fitted to the same Mark 45 mount that provides firepower on the Type 23 frigates and Type 45 destroyers. The ammunition and firing sequences can be remotely controlled from the operations room without operator intervention in the gun bay. It has a built-in test and self-diagnosis system. The gun will first be installed on board HMS GLASGOW.

114mm Vickers Mk8 Mod 1

The Royal Navy's standard medium calibre general purpose gun which arms the Type 23 frigates and Type 45 destroyers. The Mod 1 is an electrically operated version of the original gun and is recognised by its angular turret. First introduced in 2001 it is now fitted in all Type 23 and Type 45 vessels. Rate of fire: 25 rounds/min. Range: 22,000 m. Weight of Shell: 21 kg.

BOFORS 57mm Mk 3

Another new gun system that will be a feature of the future Royal Navy is the Bofors 57mm Mk3 gun system that will be the main gun armament of the Type 31 frigates. Development of this weapon started in the early 1960s in Sweden as the SjöAutomatKanon (SAK) L/70 based on the 57mm SAK L/60 built in the post-war period for several navies. This was later developed into the Mk 2 and Mk 3 by United Defence and by new owners BAE Systems. Throughout the 1980s Oto Melera 76mm mount became synonymous with naval gunnery worldwide but the Bofors system continued to be developed with a focus on accuracy, low radar cross section from its gun mount and smart 3P ammunition capability (Pre-fragmented, Programmable, Proximity-fused) rounds. The gunner can select one of six modes before firing that can shower a target with lethal airbursts of tungsten pellets, high explosive or armour piercing rounds. But at £3,800 per round Smart Ammunition is not cheap. The Bofors 57mm Mk3 has been selected by the US Coast Guard to arm its new Legend-class National Security Cutters. The system is already used by Brunei, Canada, Finland, Germany, Indonesia, Malaysia, Mexico, Norway and Sweden.

BOFORS 40mm Mk 4

The Type 31 frigates will also introduce the first 40mm gun to the Royal Navy since the Bofors 40mm L/60 Mark IX that was last used in the late 1980s. In the intervening years the Royal Navy has standardised the 30mm small calibre gun. The 40mm weapon, however, offers increased lethality against aircraft and ships and longer range. Work on the Mk 4 started in 2009 and has led to a fully digitised modularised system that is ideal for shipbuilding on a budget such as the Type 31 frigates programme. Ten mounts for the five Type 31 frigates were ordered in October 2020 with the first expected to arrive at the Rosyth shipyard later in 2023.

DS30B 30mm

Single mounting carrying an Oerlikon 30mm gun. Fitted to Type 23 frigates and various patrol vessels and MCMVs. In August 2005 it was announced that the DS30B fitted in Type 23 frigates was to be upgraded to DS30M Mk 2 to include new direct-drive digital servos and the replacement of the earlier Oerlikon KCB cannon with the ATK Mk 44 Bushmaster II 30 mm gun. Consideration is already being given to purchasing additional DS30M Mk 2 systems for minor war vessels and auxiliaries.

Phalanx CIWS

A US-built CIWS designed around the Vulcan 20 mm rotary cannon. Rate of fire is 3000 rounds/min and effective range is c.1500 m. Fitted in Type 45 and some Wave, Bay and Fort Classes. Block 1B began entering service from 2009. Incorporates side-mounted forward looking infra-red enabling CIWS to engage low aircraft and surface craft. In 2023 Babcock received a £17.9 million three-year contract from the MOD to upgrade, maintain and supply spare parts for the Royal Navy's 41 Phalanx CIWS systems. The work will be undertaken at their Devonport facility.

GAM BO 20mm

A simple hand operated mounting carrying a single Oerlikon KAA 200 automatic cannon firing 1000 rounds/min. Maximum range is 2000 m. Carried by most of the fleet's major warships except the Type 23 frigates.

20mm Mk.7A

The design of this simple but reliable weapon dates back to World War II but it still provides a useful increase in firepower, particularly for auxiliary vessels and RFAs. Rate of fire 500-800 rounds/min.

Close Range Weapons

In addition to the major weapons systems, all RN ships carry a variety of smaller calibre weapons to provide protection against emerging terrorist threats in port and on the high seas such as small fast suicide craft. In addition it is sometimes preferable, during policing or stop and search operations to have a smaller calibre weapon available. Depending upon the operational environment ships may be seen armed with varying numbers of pedestal mounted

General Purpose Machine Guns (GPMG). Another addition to the close in weapons is the Mk 44 Mini Gun, a total of 150 of which have been procured from the United States as a fleetwide fit. Fitted to a naval post mount, the Minigun is able to fire up to 3,000 rounds per minute, and is fully self-contained (operating off battery power).

DragonFire

DragonFire is the Royal Navy's £130 million directed energy weapon system programme that will be included in the weapons fit for the Type 26 frigates when they enter service. The system will also be fitted to RAF jets and to a variety of British Army combat vehicles. The first batch of the systems is currently undergoing extensive testing with lower energy outputs than production models against a variety of aerial targets. A burst of the high-intensity beam from DragonFire costs no more than £10 – yet can engage targets - drones, missiles, aircraft – at the speed of light by concentrating it on a target. The laser has been under development for nearly a decade and underwent tests by government scientists on the Ministry of Defence's ranges in the Hebrides at the start of 2024.

Torpedoes

Sting Ray

A lightweight anti-submarine torpedo which can be launched from ships, helicopters or aircraft. In effect it is an undersea guided missile with a range of 11 km at 45 knots or 7.5 km at 60 knots. Length 2.1 m, diameter 330 mm. Type 23s have the Magazine Torpedo Launch System (MTLS) with internal launch tubes. Sting Ray Mod 1 is intended to prosecute the same threats as the original Sting Ray but with an enhanced capability against small conventionally powered submarines and an improved shallow-water performance.

Spearfish

Spearfish is a submarine-launched heavyweight torpedo which has replaced Tigerfish. Claimed by the manufacturers to be the world's fastest torpedo, capable of over 70 kts, its sophisticated guidance system includes an onboard acoustic processing suite and tactical computer backed up by a command and control wire link to the parent submarine. Over 20ft in length and weighing nearly two tonnes, Spearfish is fired from the standard 21-inch submarine torpedo tube and utilises an advanced bi-propellant gas turbine engine for higher performance. The Navy is investing £270m upgrading the Spearfish heavyweight torpedo by fitting a new warhead, a safer fuel system, an enhanced electronic brain and a fibre-optic guidance link with the parent submarine in order to improve accuracy and lethality. The warhead is at least six times more powerful than that carried by the Stringray lightweight torpedo. Enhanced Spearfish will be introduced to SSNs over the next three years and will be in service until the 2050s. Sea trials have been carried out with the frigate SUTHERLAND.

At the end of the line...

• CROWN COPYRIGHT/MOD **RFA Proteus (left) and HMS Belfast**

CROWN COPYRIGHT/MOD — HMS Enterprise

HMS ECHO
Survey ship HMS ECHO's 20-year Royal Navy career formally ended on 30 June 2022 at a decommissioning ceremony at Portsmouth Naval Base. The ship was the first of two Echo-class survey ships designed for hydrographic and oceanographic operations across the world. ECHO's sister ship HMS ENTERPRISE has also ended her career. In March 2023 she was formally decommissioned from service.

HMS TALENT and HMS TRENCHANT
On 20 May 2022 in a rare double decommissioning of two Trafalgar-class nuclear powered submarines - HMS TALENT and sister submarine HMS TRENCHANT - were decommissioned at Devonport together in front of The Princess Royal, HMS TALENT's Royal patron. Both submarines served in the Royal Navy for 32-years. These two submarines joined those currently in storage at Rosyth and Devonport Dockyards awaiting demolition. Some progress has been made with the problem that has plagued successive governments - that is, what to do with the boats when they have reached the end of their service lives? In June 2023 James Cartlidge MP, Minister of State for the MoD replied to a Parliamentary question regarding the scrapping of the submarines: "Good progress continues to be made with dismantling decommissioned submarines in Rosyth. The first stage of dismantling, including the removal of all Low-Level radio-active waste, has been completed on four platforms; SWIFTSURE, RESOLUTION, REVENGE, and REPULSE." There are 22 nuclear submarines at Rosyth and Devonport awaiting disposal as of 2024.

HMS MONTROSE and HMS MONMOUTH
The UK's oldest in-service Type 23 frigates - HMS MONTROSE and HMS MONMOUTH - were declared surplus to requirement under the terms of the UK Integrated Review and Defence Command Paper. MONMOUTH decommissioned at Portsmouth on 30 June 2021 and remains laid up at the Trots in Portsmouth Harbour. Sistership MONTROSE decommissioned at Portsmouth on 17 April 2023 and also laid up in Portsmouth Harbour awaiting either sale or scrap.

CROWN COPYRIGHT/MOD HMS Cromer (in 2001)

HMS WALNEY
The Sandown-class minehunter HMS WALNEY was decommissioned in October 2010. She has been stripped of almost all useable equipment and propulsion systems while laid-up in Portsmouth Naval Base. Initially put up for sale for offers in excess of £30,000, DESA has now issued a notice of the potential sale of the former WALNEY for recycling only.

HMS CROMER
In June 2023, after many years as a static training vessel at Britannia Royal Naval College at Dartmouth, HMS CROMER was towed to Portsmouth for lay up in Basin 3 to join her Sandown-class sister ships. It is unclear, at the time of writing, whether or not CROMER will return to Dartmouth following the upgrading of the piers and jetties at the Naval College.

HMS BRISTOL
It is widely expected that BRISTOL, the sole Type 82 guided missile destroyer built, will be sold for scrap in 2024. Since the Royal Navy announced in February 2020 that the ship would no longer be used for training purposes her condition has deteriorated rapidly at her berth alongside Whale Island in Portsmouth Harbour. She commissioned into the Royal Navy in 1973 and served with distinction for 57 years including serving in the Falklands War. She is the last major British warship still afloat that fought in the South Atlantic and despite a campaign to preserve her as a museum, it seems extremely unlikely that she can be saved.

RFA WAVE KNIGHT and RFA WAVE RULER
RFA Wave Ruler has been laid up at Birkenhead since 2017 and RFA WAVE KNIGHT was laid up at Portsmouth in March 2022. In June 2023 in response to a Parliamentary question about the future of these two vessels, James Cartlidge, the Minister of State, Ministry of Defence, responded by stating that both ships were placed into Extended Readiness until 2028 in His Majesty's Naval Base Portsmouth and Liverpool respectively. He further

CROWN COPYRIGHT/MOD **Chernihiv alongside Cherkasy**

mentioned that the option to reactivate them is being reviewed. At the end of 2023 it was reported that keeping both of these ships in reserve is costing the British taxpayer between £3-4 million annually, which amounts to £12 million since they have been in reserve since 2019. Cartlidge declined to disclose the individual out-of-service dates for the ships, citing the need to preserve the operational security of the fleet, which is odd given that the department routinely discloses this information.

HMS SHOREHAM and HMS GRIMSBY
The slow run down in the fleet of minesweepers and minehunters began with the decommissioning from service of the Sandown-class minehunter HMS SHOREHAM and HMS GRIMSBY in October 2022. In September 2022, SHOREHAM was spotted operating around Firth of Forth carrying the Ukranian name CHERKASY and the pennant number M311. Though still reportedly in commission with the Royal Navy, she was training sailors of the Ukrainian Navy prior to her planned handover. Together with ex-HMS GRIMSBY (now CHERNIHIV) she was commissioned into the Ukrainian Navy on 2 July 2023 in Glasgow. In April 2024, it was announced that CHERKASY and sister ship CHERNIHIV were to be based at HMNB Portsmouth for the foreseeable future as they prepare for exercises with the Royal Navy alongside the US Navy in UK waters, which will help Ukraine understand how to operate with NATO navies.

HMS ATHERSTONE
This Hunt-class mine-countermeasures vessel was decommissioned on 14 December 2017 and has languished in Portsmouth Harbour since then gradually being stripped of parts and equipment for the surviving members of the RN Hunt Class force to keep them operational. On 3 June 2020, the stripped down ATHERSTONE was advertised for sale. Harland and Wolff shipyard bought the vessel with the intention to rebuild it as a non-military vessel or alternatively as a source of spare parts in the refit of sister ship QUORN.

CROWN COPYRIGHT/MOD

RFA Dilligence (in 2003)

HMS QUORN
The Hunt-class mine-countermeasures vessel has been purchased for refitting for the Lithuanian Navy. The £55 million contract is being undertaken by Harland and Wolff shipyard at their Appledore, North Devon shipyard. She will on completion of the refit join two sister ships in service with the Lithuanian Navy, ex-DULVERTON and ex-COTTESMORE. HMS QUORN completed 27 years of Service with the Royal Navy before being sold to Lithuania in April 2020. It is planned that the ship will be handed over to the Lithuanian Navy in 2024.

GRIFFON 2400TD LCAC
Withdrawn from Royal Marine operations is Griffon LCAC, officially known as the Landing Craft Air Cushion (Light). The so-called 'floating fortress' can carry 16 marines and race across water, ice and mud. Operated by 539 Raiding Squadron, the 2400TD offers greater payload, performance and obstacle clearance than the earlier 2000TD craft. Similiar to the 2000TD, the 2400TD's design allows the user to reduce the width of the craft with foldable side decks allowing it to be transported on a standard low loader truck or in the hold of a C-130 Hercules aircraft.

RFA DILLIGENCE
The Royal Navy's former forward repair vessel has, since 2016, been in reserve. Originally commissioned as a commercial oil rig support ship she was taken up from trade following the Falklands War, which identified the need for a forward repair ship to repair battle damaged warships in-situ and away from dockyard facilities. In 2020 a Royal Navy spokesperson said that DILLIGENCE was "an aged singleton ship with increasing obsolescence issues", and that it was no longer cost-effective to maintain her in service." The 2021 Brtish Defence White Paper made no mention of the ship or her capabilities and after a spell at Birkenhead in reserve in March 2017 she was placed within Portsmouth Dockyard where she awaited a potential buyer. In April 2023, it was revealed that the ship was to be scrapped after no suitable buyers materialised, and in March 2024 she departed the UK for the final time, under tow to a scrapyard in Turkey.